BOOKS BY
ALEXANDRA STODDARD

Alexandra Stoddard's

B O O K   O F
COLOR

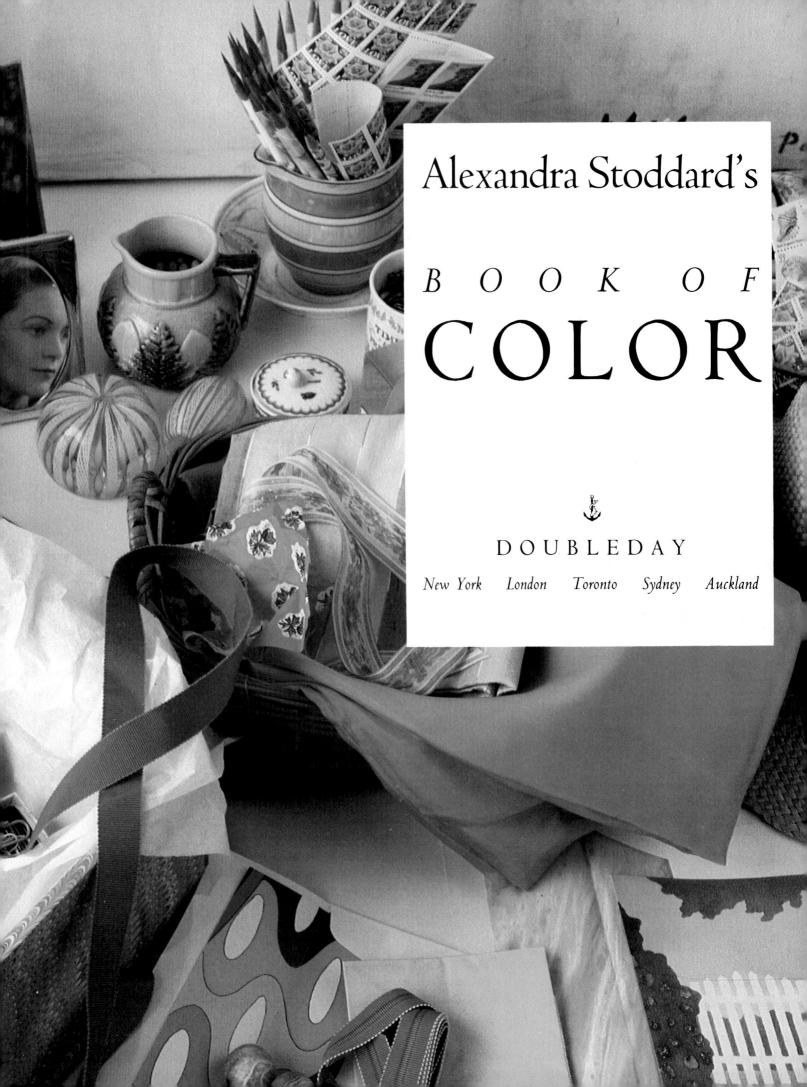

Alexandra Stoddard's

B O O K   O F
COLOR

⚓

D O U B L E D A Y

New York   London   Toronto   Sydney   Auckland

PUBLISHED BY DOUBLEDAY

a division of
Bantam Doubleday Dell Publishing Group, Inc.
666 Fifth Avenue, New York, New York 10103

DOUBLEDAY and the portrayal of an anchor with a dolphin
are trademarks of Doubleday, a division of
Bantam Doubleday Dell Publishing Group, Inc.

Library of Congress Cataloging-in-Publication Data
Stoddard, Alexandra.
[Book of color]
Alexandra Stoddard's book of color — 1st ed.
p.   cm.
ISBN 0-385-24778-8
1. Color in interior design.   2. Color—Psychology.   I. Title.
NK2115.S697   1989
747′.94—dc19   89-1558
CIP

FIRST EDITION

BOOK MARK

The text of this book was set in the typeface
Simoncini Garamond and the display
in Centaur by the Monotype Composition
Company, Baltimore, Maryland.

It was separated and printed on 70 lb
Warrenflo by Ringier America, New Berlin, Wisconsin.

DESIGNED BY MARYSARAH QUINN

To Phy Gardner, my art history teacher
from Stonleigh-Burnham School,
who sent me to art school
and introduced me to a
world of color.

ACKNOWLEDGMENTS

To Carl Brandt for his vision . . .

To Sally Arteseros for her love . . .

To Nancy Evans for her finishing touches.

CONTENTS

I

THE SPIRIT OF
COLOR

COLOR AS LANGUAGE

I first became aware that I could see and experience the delights of color when I was three years old. Before I could read or write, color was my language. It was early June (my mother later told me), and I was sitting on a narrow grass path between the borders of vividly colored flowers—geraniums, peonies, irises, oriental poppies, foxgloves, and roses—and I became transformed. As I sat on the grass, some of the flowers seemed tall as trees; when I stood, many of them were way over my head. I stared at the color of these flowers in deep contemplation . . . I didn't have words to describe the rich plum of the iris or the hot magenta of the geraniums or the fragile, pale pink of the peonies. I connected and became one with these living colors and they communicated to me a special vocabulary that has sustained me all my life.

Before I could read I was fully aware of the messages color conveyed. Because of this powerful initial moment of awareness I can take myself back to being in the garden that June morning forty-three years ago. I was wearing a pink-and-white smocked seersucker sundress and had a pink grosgrain ribbon in my hair. Since this dramatic moment of my first memory, when I became aware of my own physical and spiritual color consciousness, I have seen the world: I've traveled to Russia, all over Europe, to the

Scandinavian countries, to exotic Asia, Africa, the Near and Far East. Because of my passion for color, I feel comfortable in every country; I intuitively sense the spirit, the pulse, the essence of where I am—places speak to me through color. It was in Bali that I realized that color is only possible because of light. At 4:15 A.M. we awoke and had breakfast, watching the sun rise over the milky green ocean. How can you sleep when all those changing colors await your discovery?

When I had my first color memory, we lived in a sprawling 150-year-old yellow farmhouse in Weston, Massachusetts. Next to the house was an old red barn, and surrounding both the house and barn were tall trees, flowers, and ancient stone walls. I began absorbing colors when I helped my mother in her flower garden, which introduced me to a special world of color. The memory of this experience brings me joy every day I live.

When I was seven I had my own garden. We had moved to Connecticut when I was five and had a farm in New York State where we went in the summer. Mother arranged for a local farmer to plow a plot for me after she helped me stake out my garden. After four years of apprenticeship in

ALEXANDRA STODDARD'S

Mother's garden I felt I knew how to design my own. What began as a sweet gesture on my mother's part turned into an all-consuming passion for me. I combined flowers, fruits, and vegetables so that everywhere I looked my eye was stimulated and my senses delighted. The colors of fruit, vegetables and flowers, personally planted and nurtured, have given me a wider understanding of the magical qualities color holds for each of us. I am still in awe of the vast vocabulary and dimension that color freely offers us. Colors can stir our emotions, change our moods, touch our hearts, expand our vision. It can open all our senses—our taste buds, our sense of smell and touch; we can see the world in the most wondrous ways.

I believe we can learn how to bring these fresh, delicious colors into our hearts and live with their clear, crisp beauty every day in our houses, apartments, and places of work. We can learn how to see and appreciate color in a new and personal way by remembering the simple rituals we performed in childhood—playing in the red barn, skipping barefoot to avoid the sprinkler on new spring grass, eating watermelon outdoors, flying colorful kites, crayoning, holding a yellow balloon. I have never lost my childlike wonder of the immense pleasure color can bring. Color feeds my soul and continually rejuvenates my spirit, and when I envision form, I always see it in color. It is color that shapes my visual world and influences my emotions. I have made color a priority and a friend because I am totally aware of its power for me. I understand myself through color. Whether from nature or art or from harmonious schemes created by man, color is that magical experience that gives me an inspirational and spiritual life.

Color, as I learned about it through my passion for flowers and gardening, is the single reason I became an interior designer. By the time I was nine, after two summers as a "professional" gardener, I had my career all mapped out—I was going to be a horticulturist. My mother loved studying seed catalogues and I read these in the winter along with her. I collected seed packages, anticipating the new birth of nature's miracles in the spring. Mother and I would sit by the fire on a cold winter's night and discuss our gardens.

In the winter I learned how to envision the abundance of spring. Yet I sensed there was something inconsistent with my flower-inspired vision and the way people actually lived with color.

COLOR DEPRIVATION

When I was a child, the interior of the houses in our neighborhood in Connecticut seemed dark and dreary. People closed their curtains so the colors of their fabrics and carpeting wouldn't fade. Neighbors actually sat in their rooms on sunny days with their curtains fully closed. Houses, from the inside, felt like morgues. I remember the feeling of going inside a friend's house on a sunny summer's day. It became a mini-death for me and was frightening. I grew to learn that this darkness had little to do with money, but was the result of an emotional attitude that valued preservation and conservation instead of celebration of the moment. How glorious it would have been for those neighbors to live inside sun-drenched rooms and let their fabrics mellow naturally in time!

I pondered why so many people lived in drab, dull houses. Where were the life and light? Where was the energy, the joy? Where were the sparkle and the fresh clear colors from nature? The beauty and happiness of the sunny summer's day was blocked out, like a candle that's been blown out. Being inside these colorless, closeted houses was like experiencing a gray, dreary, rainy day, and it made me feel sad. I knew color could make a difference.

Do older people naturally lose their love of fresh colors, I wondered. When they put their crayons away do they forget about the joy fresh color brought them in the past? I found I couldn't stop questioning why so many architecturally charming houses were dark and depressingly heavy inside. All I remember is an overwhelming sense of brown and dull green-gray. I couldn't imagine people really feeling uplifted and joyous in such dreary rooms. If I found them tired, I wondered, how could others find them delightful?

My mother explained to me that when people are older they tend to have more subtle and soothing colors around them because those colors are more sophisticated—more formal, more "proper." Yet I felt a loss—of opportunity as well as of vitality. Children lived in those houses too.

Suddenly, when I was in fifth grade, like turning on a light, I decided to switch careers! I'd leave horticulture for others—gardens didn't need me. They were out of doors in sunny places—they had a real advantage over enclosed, interior places. I decided my mission was to become an interior decorator so I could attempt to bring the colors I'd grown to love from my garden inside. I followed in the path where my mother had so thoughtfully led me. I was determined to bring a garden-soaked color palette into the homes where we really spend most of our lives.

My mother, an amateur decorator, instinctively joined her love of

nature and gardening to the color choices she made inside our house. I too grew to need these colors to support me in the winter; I wanted the indoors to be a continuation of the garden in the spring and summer. I felt others must also need those happy colors in order to feel cheerful. Mother had a natural flair for decorating and an avid interest in houses. Once all four of her children were in school all day, she drove an hour to New Haven to Yale several times a week to study architecture and design. After receiving some formal education, Mother became a partner in an attractive shop in Westport called Country Interior Designers. What she was doing primarily for herself was also instructing me through example. When other children were playing with dolls, I would go to her studio and play with floral chintzes, color harmonies, and delectably colored fabric and paint swatches. This experience, coupled with my exposure to gardens, hooked me to the magic and joy of color at an impressionable age.

ASSOCIATIONS

I discovered I instinctively made happy color associations based on my earlier inspiration from nature. Scientists are now linking color with memory, believing that color sends signals to the brain. The taste of an apple together with the color red strengthens the synapses between neurons. As I looked at the color samples I automatically associated them with flowers, fruit, vegetables, grass, trees, sky, water. I arranged them together the way I would plan my garden. This useful recreation taught me that I could actually improve my mood by having color relationships that I associated with good memories.

As a professional decorator I have realized that all of the pleasure and beauty I have experienced with colors in nature can be transported inside. Walls, floors, furniture, sheets, towels, quilts, china—all can have the spirit of a sunny garden or a carefree day at the beach. I've spent most of my life trying to achieve these effects. I can actually walk into my husband's and my bedroom and feel I am walking on the beach on a sun-drenched August afternoon. Wood floors can be bleached a sand color. I have learned that if you paint your ceiling a perfect sky blue and your walls a shiny white with Emalj paint, you will be reminded of the white foam of waves. Or your living room can have a hint of lilac on the walls to remind you of early June when the air smells of lilacs and you can look forward to a summer spent mostly out of doors.

The French textile designer Manuel Canovas understands all of this.

Once, while sitting on a terrace in France, he looked down into a monk's garden filled with an abundance of sweet peas in pink, yellow, white, lilac, and fresh baby green, and he was inspired to draw exactly what he saw. He created one of my favorite flower chintzes, called Joy, which we now have in our bedroom. Flower chintzes can bring the spirit of your garden inside your house. By sprinkling a flowered chintz around a room—on curtains, on upholstered furniture, or on your bed—you can experience the mood of a sun-drenched garden. You and the garden become one. There are hundreds of other ways to do this. Wallpaper can be garden-inspired, or your art can be botanical prints. You can collect porcelain fruits and vegetables and your color scheme can be springlike. Keeping flowering plants and fresh-cut flowers in the rooms where you spend time makes the garden flow inside.

When I was growing up in Westport we had a gigantic pink magnolia tree perfuming our front yard. As a little girl I would lie under this pink umbrella in April and look up at the sky through the blossoms, transfixed. All these years later I have the most vivid memories of being enveloped by that magnificent pink burst, and all around me were the fallen scented petals contrasted against the new spring grass. Because of this childhood attraction to being enveloped by nature's colors, pink, green, and blue are especially satisfying to me. Inspired by my love of lying under the magnolia tree, I designed a rug combining those three colors for a New York apartment that has an exceptional view of Central Park.

I also remember generous amounts of pale pink peonies, which were

my favorite bloom around the end of May. Now our living-room walls in New York are lacquered this delicate peony color, and when I walk into our living room I feel the essence of spring, of peonies, and of the fresh, perfumed air that magical time of year suggests. Watering our two lemon trees with a huge watering can brings back to me the pleasant childhood memory of watering the flowers in my garden. I equate fresh, clear colors with radiant health and vitality.

PASSIONS

Now that I am an adult, I have not changed my color vision at all. In fact, what started out to be a childhood passion has become a way of thinking and living. I am in love with certain colors. I've learned we all should color our private worlds with the most personal, the sweetest and the freshest colors we can find. I have a friend who likes fluffy colors because they make her happy. Fluffy colors (frothy pink, mossy green) are light as air. I've discovered that when we do express our passion for our favorite colors, we open ourselves up to nostalgic memories, to fresh hope and grace. Our mood and attitude improve when we consciously select colors that satisfy us emotionally. The atmosphere is elevated when we open ourselves up to the radiance of the pure, beautiful colors we love. When we personalize our colors, we are deliberately using color to express ourselves. When we do this we usually create an atmosphere others find attractive and appealing. Color is amazingly revealing. Color represents us, whether we like it or not, and by paying attention to color we can keep in touch with our own feelings as well as the feelings of others.

My intense love of color has taught me how to see. It is a known fact that a child develops the ability to see by distinguishing contrasts—brightness and darkness. Next is movement and then shape and form. The recognition of color is the last development. Seeing color, distinguishing colors, and reacting aesthetically are the result of education and development, not instinct. Color, however, is the first thing adults perceive, and it speaks louder than form. But when I see the Acropolis, I don't yell, "Ah, beige! My favorite color!" as Elsie de Wolfe, the first "professional" American interior designer is supposed to have said when viewing it for the first time. I experience the columns of the Parthenon in relationship to the sky, and the blue void between the spaces draws me to the majestic tapering of the fluted marble Doric columns.

The more you enjoy color, the more you experiment and play with color, the more you will perceive it around you. The colors you now love and identify with are extremely personal. They are intimate references from your past and they are an outward symbol of your interior world. For example, the flower colors I fell in love with as a child bring me fresh happiness every time I experience them in natural settings or in man-made environments. All of my happiest memories and moments of awareness are color-associated.

The same is true of sad moments. I've learned to use positive memory colors to create cheerful, appealing emotions and to shy away from colors that have sad, unpleasant personal associations. I have a friend who often

wears a harsh golden green sweater and it reminds me of the Vietnam War. I associate that particular shade of color with camouflage fatigues, with war, battle, bloodshed, and agony. There is a particular dull turquoise blue that I associate with the walls of the hospital room where I once had to spend a lot of time. I shudder when I see that color; I feel fear of physical and emotional pain. The worst aspect of our family trip to Leningrad was the color deprivation we felt there. The only color I remember that relieved the depressing grayness was the red of the Communist flag.

COLOR SENSE

When we express color symbolically it becomes autobiography. Our color palette expresses our individual personality and outlook on life. Be guided by how you react to colors emotionally, because your reaction can give you meaningful clues. For instance, you may still be surrounded by the colors your mother liked. But are they really the colors you like? Thousands of color tests indicate that color stimulates every individual, regardless of background or personality, in the same way. Red will universally stimulate people in a similar manner. You may love red, and I may want it in small doses. We are different personalities and it is our individual response to color that should guide us as we try to keep our lives in balance. Once you become aware of the colors you want to live with, you can make wise choices based solely on trusting your instincts. You will have bodily reactions to specific colors, as to all strong emotional experiences. Understanding this makes us aware of how we respond to all the colors in our private world at home.

The colors we select to represent us—and color does speak for us—should be selected purely because they delight our spirit. I know I have a strong need for colors to be wondrous and alive, like sunshine dappling through the lacy leaves of a beautiful tree. I like to fantasize that my daily life can be lived in a color palette as original as scenes from Impressionist paintings.

No matter how much you study color theory, no one can teach you what colors are the ones for you to live with, because your taste is as individual as your thumbprint. If colors don't satisfy you deep inside, they are not right for you. Try to make sure that the colors you choose to live with have positive, healthy associations, so that you will enjoy your colors in a joyous way.

An un-joyous example is the true story of a husband who ordered two expensive Italian natural brown leather sofas through a top California interior designer. When they arrived his wife cried in anger, "Get them out of here. They remind me of cow dung! I could never sit on them." This is a sad color-reaction story. The lady was raised on a Texas farm and that particular natural shade of leather triggered that association. If only this couple had communicated better, they could have picked a leather color both could enjoy—deep hunter green or burgundy or rich French blue. Once you rate colors by associations, you can choose personally uplifting colors for your home, your wardrobe, and all the corners of your life. You instinctively will be repelled by certain colors regardless of their status, expense, or sophistication. By relating colors to memories, you train your eye to envision those special moments that have delighted you, and you will always react honestly to color.

Look at the world through your own specially colored lens. Each of us sees colors in our own way because of our experiences. When we live with someone and share a color palette, we must communicate our likes and dislikes so that the two palettes merge into a positive harmony. The husband's dream to own those $8,000 natural brown leather sofas turned out to be his wife's nightmare. She insisted they had to go or she would. That was an expensive color error which cost great emotional pain. But ultimately, no matter how much you love another person, it is perfectly possible that you can't live with certain colors.

Never be dictated to by people selling you color. The popular earth tones would dampen my spirit. The punchy primaries would make me

nervous. My gentle pastel palette might put you to sleep. Through trial and error you will make your own color discoveries, and what is fascinating is that the colors that flatter your skin tone and the colors you select to have around you in your rooms are all part of a whole color palette.

Colors that appeal to you intimately, much in the same way you are chemically drawn to another person, are your colors. I don't wear gold colors nor do I decorate with gold. I have a consistent color palette and it strives for clear, fresh pigments. I have a love affair with unsophisticated colors. Just as a healthful diet is both good for you and can be a delicious adventure into the tasty foods you adore, finding the colors you are drawn to can improve your health, your spirit, and your sense of personal satisfaction. Finding your own color palette is like finding your essence. When you do you will feel whole.

POWER

Once we become open to and aware of the power of color, it will bring us grace and serenity, and we will be able to transform the places we live and work into real extensions of our best selves. Color provides you with your inner equilibrium. If you are in need of physical regeneration you will instinctively choose blue to soothe you. Color can be here for you today, and if you decide tomorrow that you no longer like a color, you can change it. Use color as your instrument, much in the way that a violinist uses his. With practice you will learn to touch a particular nerve by combining certain chords of harmonious colors. When we use color as a way of expressing our love of life, we can experiment and play with color—dabble—and experience moments of ecstasy.

Over more than twenty-five years as a professional interior designer, I have been fascinated by the impact people's personal color choices have on their mood and outlook. Once we examine where we are in our color journey, recognizing and identifying our current color preferences, we will be eager to express this unique palette and will be faithful to it as long as it feels good. Our color sense—and it is a sense—will change over the span of our lives in much the same way that an artist stretches for new directions. Emotional maturity will change our reaction to certain colors we were once attracted to, but we should try to look for the bright clarity in each color we select, so they are pure, clean, and refreshing.

Discover new color combinations by experimentation and observation. Find fresh new delights by editing colors you've outgrown. Be open to the wonders of color for you. Stretch yourself to fresh inspiration. The more pleasure you get from color's magical gifts, the more you will recognize

your need to express yourself through your own color palette. Feel free to go through your "blue period" and, if the spirit moves you, go on to a new color phase. Try to embrace new lovely colors that surprise you. It is a fringe benefit that we tend to have a wider vision when we are physiologically, psychologically, and spiritually pleased.

One of the most interesting aspects of my design work is helping clients to translate their happy color-associated memories into their current surroundings. I try to help people think of color in non-stereotyped ways. By learning about their memories and what experiences make them happy, I am able to help them translate these sensuous feelings. Appreciating fresh fruit, vegetable, and flower colors should not have a male-female association. Dark, rich, absorbing colors—red, burgundy, hunter green, mahogany brown, black, and dark blue—considered "masculine" colors—are appreciated by females as well as males. Avoid color "myths." Some men adore pink and some women are wild about dark green. Tommy T. B. Koh, the ambassador to the United States from Singapore, hired me because he liked my sense of color. "People think that because I'm an ambassador I need dark, rich, serious colors. I like pastel colors." Sensitivity, associations, chemistry, and your emotional reaction—not your sex—determine your color preferences.

I have clients who have separate studies in their home: hers is red and his is pale blue. She gets energy from her red walls and he is soothed by his blue. Louis XIV wasn't worried about his masculinity when he created the color schemes for Versailles. It did not occur to a Roman emperor wearing a robe of Tyrian purple, causing hundreds of thousands of snails to give their lives, whether purple was masculine or feminine. The emperor wanted to wear a color no one else could obtain. I have a client who always wears pink socks. He has a drawerful of pink socks.

EXPRESSION

Have self-confidence and enjoy expressing your personal color palette. A woman makes a big mistake to assume that a man would feel out of place in a pale pink bedroom or living room. After a man divorced his wife, his house was redone to reflect his own color palette, which was fresh from his garden. His ex-wife, who was unhappy, had had a dull, neutral color scheme for their house. Brown and gray are signs of timidity, and studies indicate they are the colors of people who are physically and spiritually exhausted. Neutral gray, where there is a balance between white and black, is a total

void of color, like living life inside a black-and-white movie or in a continuous rainstorm. Healthy people—male and female—respond to refreshing, pretty, clear colors because they represent light and sunshine.

I find that unmarried men as well as divorced men are articulate when they describe scenes in their lives—moods they want to re-create. If a man is an avid gardener, it is logical that his house will be filled with flowers and all the colors he adores from his garden. When I work with married couples I interview the spouses individually to be certain I hear accurately what colors each adores and which they hate. I also interview each child separately. Some of the best color schemes are the result of combining favorite colors from two or more people with different color palettes. Take someone who likes blue and white and add another person's bottle green, plum, and touches of yellow.

Because the colors we choose have to do with our personalities, those we enjoy wearing are the ones that make us look and feel terrific. We must never be afraid and play it safe with color. Holding back—being color-conservative—I call "hiding behind beige." When we can't decide what we really want, we make a non-decision and pick beige—the color of the poor

ALEXANDRA STODDARD'S

of yesterday who had to be content to wear unbleached cloth because organic dyes were too expensive. We can't afford to be passive about color because if we are, we will feel dragged down and we will lose our vitality. Listen for clues: Being color-passive is like wearing a mask, observing life from a distance.

HOW TO MAKE PERSONAL COLOR CHOICES

Color is alive, intimate, and immediate! For a man, the color of his necktie makes an important statement. For others, the color of his necktie communicates his current mood. This is one of the few opportunities a man has to show off his color flair in his clothes. The silk scarf he tucks into his blazer pocket is a signal. His shirt, suit, shoes, and socks can be subtle color messages. These decisions will make a difference in his mood and self-confidence. Once a man feels comfortable wearing colors he enjoys, he will also want them expressed in his apartment or house and place of work.

The color of your bed covers, your towels, rugs, walls, tiles, your fabrics, furniture, pottery, porcelain, your flowers—these color decisions are made in much the same way that you select a lipstick, powder, or nail polish, a nightgown, a skirt, pajamas, or a blouse. You select colors that

are appropriate—either to your skin tone in the case of clothing, or the scheme of your room when decorating. But always select from a range of your own favorite colors. Choose a tablecloth, a shower curtain, or a napkin by the impact of its color on your spirit as well as by how suitable it is with the surrounding colors. When a man has a suit custom-made, the color of the cloth is established first and then the cut and fit are worked out according to what looks best on his body. When I look for a dress, I am first attracted by color and then I examine the line and see what looks best on me.

I want what I eat to be as appealing as possible in its coloration. Before sampling the flavor of food, we are enormously influenced by the color presentation. Yellow corn on the cob reminds us of long summer days and being barefoot, tan, relaxed, and carefree. Yellow triggers our brains to associate corn on the cob with earlier experiences of enjoying it.

When planning a meal you can picture that a beautiful, colorful "still

life" of food will taste delicious because all the senses are engaged and alert. Whatever you serve, try to have colors that pique the appetite. If I'm serving Maryland crab, for example, I'll place it on several different green lettuce varieties and have slivers of lemon and lime as garnish. While most people plan meals around taste and nutrition, I think of a menu as a color scheme that is pretty. Then I focus on the things that are tasty, seasonal, and nutritious in that color range. We eat colors! And because this is true, our sense of color and taste can enhance and awaken our appetites not only for food but for life. By opening up our memory to a special meal we've savored we can recall a past pleasure for years to come.

The memory of fresh homemade peach ice cream we ate on an August evening thirty years ago whets our appetite and makes us hungry for this gentle fresh color and flavor. I can never see a certain shade of pink without remembering the smell, taste, and fun of trading bubble-gum cards and blowing huge bubbles that friends would pop. A certain shade of deep purple reminds me of our grape arbor and the fun of making fresh grape juice and jelly. When I use a grape shade of ink I can smell and taste the essence of grape as I write. A certain vibrant yet delicate shade of red

reminds me of slicing a ripe tomato I'd grown and making a tomato sandwich with bread my mother had freshly baked that had a rich, thick crust and a hint of honey flavor.

Once you've had breakfast on a sunny terrace where a pot of marmalade

ALEXANDRA STODDARD'S

captures the sunlight and you have the leisure to sit quietly and nibble on a fresh croissant, sipping dark rich coffee from a hand-painted cup—every time you see that particular shade of pale orange, you will associate it with this memory and with the soothing bittersweet taste of marmalade. You will remember the morning when you had time to see color in a special way.

Next to my childhood passion for nature, especially for flowers, I had an intense interest in art and design. This was stimulated by my mother and godmother, who exposed me at an early age to the best museums in Massachusetts, Connecticut, and New York. I saw my first Impressionist paintings at the Boston Fine Arts Museum when I was five and was captivated by their ability to evoke the pleasure of the fleeting moment outdoors in another age a hundred years ago. Claude Monet, my favorite Impressionist painter, said he was good for nothing except painting and gardening. At the end of his life he confessed he owed a great deal of his success as an artist to his passion for gardening. Georges Clemenceau, the great World War I statesman, characterized his friend Monet as "the painter of light."

Monet's paintings taught me not to look at the surface of things but to look into their depths. At the end of his life when he was almost blind he painted the water lily gardens he had created at Giverny; one can see a riot of colors under the surface of the still water.

As we enlarge and discover our own color palettes we can imitate the Impressionists and go outside into nature to experience the charm of changing light and color. The Impressionists were individualists and so are we. We too can break preconceived color rules. . . . We can find and be ourselves in the world of the color spectrum.

II

T H E

SPECTRUM

WHAT IS THE COLOR SPECTRUM?

Sunlight dispersed through a triangular glass prism displays the color spectrum. White light is broken into its parts and the result is different bands of hues in the identical order of a natural rainbow: red, orange, yellow, green, blue, violet. The spectrum can also be seen in a bubble, a cobweb, or in oil spilled in a puddle of water. The spectrum we actually see is a narrow band within an infinitely wider spectrum of electromagnetic radiation. Each color in the spectrum of light has a different wavelength. For example, red has the longest and brightest wavelengths and purple the shortest. Brightness is energy.

Light is energy radiation that includes all colors. Color is a sensory perception, brought to us by certain energy rays of light. When we are in a position to understand our environment optically, this stimulus gives information to the eye and brain.

The three primary colors are red, yellow, and blue. They cannot be obtained by any mixing. These three primary colors—in various combinations of hue, value, tint, tone, and shade—make up all the other colors in the spectrum. The three secondary colors (the colors between the primaries) are orange, green, and violet. The secondary colors are made up of about equal portions of two of the primary colors. Red and yellow create orange.

Blue and yellow create green. Red and blue create violet. To help in our exploration of color, here are definitions of some key color terms.

Hue: A hue is a color—red, orange, yellow, green, blue, or violet. Take one hue and mix it with another, and you change the hue. Red plus green becomes a red-green.

Value: The brightness or lightness of a color is its value. The three primaries (red, yellow, blue) have the strongest chromatic value of all colors in the spectrum.

Tint: White added to a primary or a secondary color lightens it. Red tinted with a large portion of white creates pink.

Shade: Black added to a primary or secondary color darkens it. Add black to orange and eventually it becomes brown.

Tone: Mix black and white in about equal portions and you create gray. Add gray to any primary or secondary color and you tone the color down. This lessens the intensity (brightness) of the color.

LIGHT

The Greek word for light is *phaos*. Light is composed of photons, or pockets of energy. Light is what allows us to experience the miracle of color. The first phenomenon of the world was light. Light generates all colors. Color and light are intimately related because without light there would be no color. The great English landscape artist John Constable reminds us, "The sky is the source of light in nature and governs everything." Each of us can relate to this personally because we are all greatly affected by bad weather. Our spirits, on the other hand, are lifted when the sun shines on us. Scientists have discovered that light deprivation can cause serious depression. People who suffer from S.A.D. (Seasonal Associated Disorder) can be cured by light therapy. Some people wear specially tinted lenses so they will feel better. In bright sunlight all colors sparkle. The dappled light filtering through trees, grass, flowers and through the windows of our homes colors our moods and thoughts. Light is life, energy, activity. Yale University's motto is *lux et veritas*—light and truth. Light is pure and good; it warms us and enhances our sense of well-being. In the dark of winter, when we are cold and starved for light, we instinctively light candles and sit by the warmth of fires, thinking about spring which is new light.

Once when Claude Monet was working on "Woman in the Garden" (one of my favorite paintings—a lady in a long white dress is surrounded by green, with touches of red flowers), his friend Gustave Courbet questioned him: Why was he holding a paintbrush in his hand and not painting? Monet's logical explanation is memorable. "I'm waiting for the sun."

An English photographer and his assistant flew to Paris for a week of photographing a house I'd decorated. A whole week went by and nothing happened until *suddenly* the sun came out on the last day and there was the picture of the sun beaming down on the house and walled garden.

We, in turn, can use color to express the exuberance we feel when we are in sun-drenched rooms full of natural light. Fresh clear colors seem to have an inner light. We can select, from thousands of different color hues distinguishable by the human eye, our own colors that express our own light from within. Before we look at individual colors, let's start with white.

WHITE

Think of white as the receiver of color. White is a perfect color because it is a symbol of purity. White is composed of the entire spectrum of colors, and is important when we build our color palettes because its bright radiance enhances all colors. White is associated with refinement, delicacy, and high expectations. White is the color of mourning in China. My friend Joan Brady, an accomplished watercolor artist, once told me something I'll never forget. An art teacher told her when she first began to paint that she should think of her white paper as light. This revolutionized my thinking because white can represent inner light. I subsequently learned that any color that doesn't look good against white is a muddy color.

White is light and must radiate outward through all colors. White brings sparkle inside where we live. Never be afraid of white. Because white is light, it can never be cold. White reaches out and overflows the physical boundaries of space. Think of how open space appears after a blanket of fresh snow has fallen. As white light contains all the colors of the spectrum it is charged with energy. White, like light, will bring you energy too. "In visual perception a color is almost never seen as it really is—as it physically is," Josef Albers wrote in *Interactions of Color*. We never see white, or light, in isolation. All colors in nature are tinted by their neighboring colors. Because of this, I usually trim all my clients' windows and woodwork with the shiniest lacquer white Emalj paint so that natural light bounces inside and enlivens all the surrounding colors. White allows us to experience luminous color.

My husband Peter's and my bed hangings are swags of white embroidered linen that suggest the lace of vigorous waves tumbling to shore. White is always refreshing to the spirit because white light is purifying. Don't start out with off-white. "Off" means what it is—off. Once you understand that white is light and all colors are included in white, you will want to keep white pure. Think of chalk white and a fresh snowfall. A client called a paint contractor and asked him to paint the entire inside of her house "chalk white." The painter searched all the paint company charts and found a "chalk white" that was, in truth, a greenish-gray off-white. While the client was away the entire inside of her house was painted an ugly, off-white. Ask for pure-white paint and be sure you see a sample. Pure-white pigment receives the surrounding colors. White tones down in time, but the clear dream of a spanking-new beginning should be *pure*, unadulterated white. There is nothing more refreshing to my spirit than a newly opened gardenia—its white is the purest, its scent the most nostalgic, and it reminds me of my first party corsage, worn on my left shoulder over thirty years ago. I write on bright white paper, and the whiteness is as important to me as the smooth surface for my pen flowing with colored ink.

I think of white as a crisp, clear, sparkling day or as skiing after a fresh fall of powder snow. White is light, purity, and *goodness*. White gives us a clean start. White gives me the feeling of lightness of being—gossamer white embroidered curtains billowing in fresh breezes, making dancelike patterns against the floor, walls, and ceiling. White is young, fresh, vital, and innocent. Like a radiant bride dressed in white, holding a nosegay of lilies of the valley, white is radiant health and hope. White is our blank canvas, our sheet of watercolor paper ready for garden-fresh pigment to be added. White is our pad of writing paper ready to receive colorful stories and images. A white can of spray starch implies that it will make ironing easier. White is pure linen bed sheets crisply ironed, ready for tenderness and love. White is opportunity.

Once you experience white, what are the colors you want to add to your canvas? Let's take some steps together and study the spectrum colors objectively, because studies prove that the "structure" of color is constant and each color means the same thing symbolically to all of us. Then we can respond individually and see color from our own personal vision. The three primary colors mixed together with white are all that is necessary for you and me to create our personal color palettes.

When you examine the three primary and three secondary colors of the spectrum individually—red, orange, yellow, green, blue, and violet— take time to observe your psychological and physiological reaction to each of them. Each color has its own emotional overtone. You will find, by study and experimenting, which colors you are most comfortable with, at what intensity, and how best to disperse them.

RED: A PRIMARY COLOR

Red sits proudly on top of the rainbow and is the color of vitality, strength, nobility, rank, and power. Red is no color for sissies. Red is among the oldest color names. Red was extracted from plants and insects and mined from the earth to paint the skins of early man. To ancient man, blood held the secret of life and was credited with special powers. In China the word "blood" is older than "red."

Of all the colors in the spectrum, red has the greatest emotional impact. How do you respond to red? Red is force, vigor, and energy. Red's emotional content is desire and it symbolizes fire. Red reaches our heart, flesh, and emotion. Experiments show that this color has a stimulating effect on the nervous system and that it increases brain activity. Red causes blood pressure to increase and quickens the heart rate. It prompts the release of adrenaline into the bloodstream. In China and Bolivia the bride wears red—the color of sex, love, and joy. Red is also associated with the planet Mars, with war and demons, and danger. Insect killers are packaged in red. Red is considered the color of passion and sexuality, of activity and conquest.

There are certain feelings people have in common when they experience red. Red expands life and is exciting, aggressive, warm, and vital. Time seems to go by faster and objects seem bigger and heavier because red appears dense. Red-hot and heart-pounding, red stirs our blood. William Butler Yeats says red is the color of magic in every country.

Red has the connotation of winning and success, of love and excess. Red charges the spirits. People are given the "red-carpet treatment." A "scarlet woman" in Puritan times was an adulteress branded with a scarlet letter. The "red-light" district sends out signals. Our hearts are red as in St. Valentine's Day hearts. Our blood races when we "see red." Teachers use red to correct students' papers. Egyptians marked headings of important events or good dreams in red ink. The Christian church used red to show feasts in the ecclesiastical calendar—"red-letter days."

Vermilion red, the prerogative of power, was the color Emperor K'ang Hsi of China, who sat on the dragon throne for sixty-one years, used to write his edicts. A red book jacket catches your eye in a bookstore. We think of crimson, scarlet, carmine, vermilion, and cinnabar. Red is the color for the Indian goddess of beauty and wealth as well as for the warrior. In religious symbolism red was the favorite color of medieval dress, epitomizing courage and purity. Red is an impulsive color and stimulates our cravings, including our appetites, which is why many restaurants decorate with red. This is a color that is attractive to people who value intensity and fullness in all aspects of their lives.

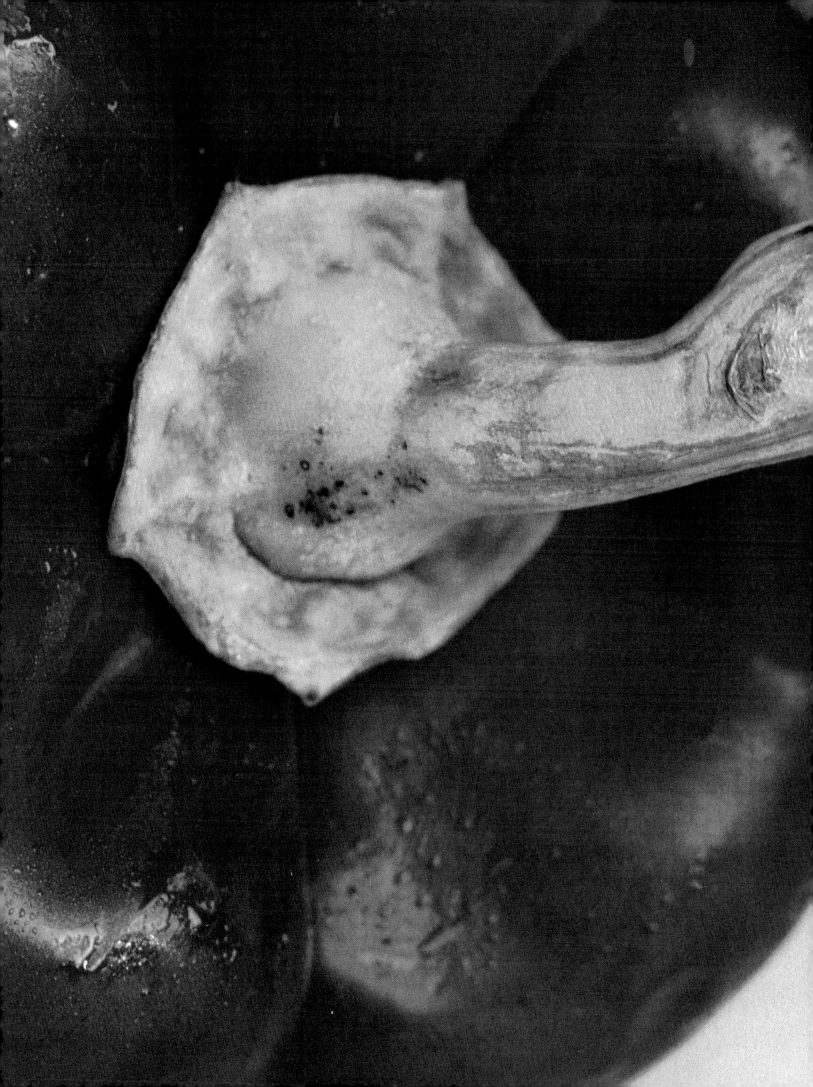

The coach Knute Rockne of Notre Dame would take his football team into a blindingly red room at half time and inspire them to get in there and fight. Red is a symbol of competition and the will to win. They'd go back into the field with renewed self-confidence and strength and make touchdowns. Red is the hottest of warm colors and the nearest in wavelength to infrared, which produces the sensation of heat. Babies put into red environments, however, become agitated and nervous and cry more than when they're in soothingly colored rooms, yet red is the first color they perceive. Children use up red crayons first, but in a red classroom they become argumentative.

Your subjective responses to color will be contradictory and you should never disregard them. Red walls can be reassuring or discomforting, depending on your personality and emotional state. I have a wine-red room I use as an office and it stimulates me to work hard. Diana Vreeland's red library is legend and suits her strong personality. I drink red wine in the winter because psychologically it warms my blood. Santa Claus wears a red costume. Tabasco sauce is red-hot. Small red peppers are hot. When we

ALEXANDRA STODDARD'S

are angry we turn red. Red advances, making objects seem nearer than they truly are. Internationally, red is the color that signals danger. Rubies are red, so are fire engines and the blood of conquest. If you wear a red dress people remember you *and* the red dress. You stand out in a crowd. Men wear red neckties on television. Revolution is red. Fire extinguishers are red. Red ink is a warning, and when you're overdrawn you are "in the red." Lipstick and nail polish are in shades of red. Poinsettias are red. Some tulips and some geraniums are red. Tomatoes, radishes, beets, and cherries are red. Watermelon is red. How much red do you have in your home? Your office? How much red do you wear?

When I think about red and nature, I realize that pure red occupies a small percentage of the whole landscape. While I've been in forests of flaming azaleas, they have been pink-and-white mixtures, and pink is toned-down red. Pink is tenderness, love, sweetness, and communion. Pink is acquiescent, gentle, and changes gender to feminine. We should remember that baby pink is red with a lot of white, which is light. Bougainvillea is purple-red. My logo for my design firm is geranium red and my shopping bag is red, so it sends a strong signal and can't be missed. Red has the power to command attention. That's why it is the safety color for stop signs and lights. I use red not in large doses, but to accent and punctuate. My Filofax organizer book is red; so is my change purse so I can see it easily when I reach into my pocketbook. I have some red reading glasses and they give me energy on rainy days. A red umbrella on a rainy day puts a smile on my face. I have a wide-brimmed red straw hat that gives my face a rosy glow. But when you decorate with red it is more permanent—red is hot.

When used with discretion, red adds to the fullness and intensity of our lives. Red is the exclamation mark, the self-confidence, the spice that gives us snap, vitality, and all the wonders of a full life.

ORANGE: A SECONDARY COLOR

The name of the color orange is linked in many languages with the fruit of the orange tree. The French adorned brides with orange blossoms, which symbolized hope of fruitfulness. Orange is cheerful, extroverted, expansive, contemporary, and young. You mix yellow and red to create orange, so this color is warm, rich, strong, and vital. Orange has no negative associations. Oranges, cantaloupes, luxurious mangoes, persimmons, peaches, and papaya. In classical times the seeds of pomegranates were thought to be an aphrodisiac. A field of daylilies, an Orange Crush, a popsicle, marmalade. Orange yams, squash, and carrots. October pumpkins and autumn leaves, roaring fires in the hearth, exotic spices—curry, gleaming copper, a Buddhist monk's saffron robe, a Howard Johnson roof, nasturtium. "Red" hair is orange. Orange can have a strong temper. Orange has drama and intensity.

Looking back at the rooms I decorated twenty years ago, I discover lots of orange. Looking at color photographs, I see I wore a great deal of orange in my twenties. As a child, just seeing the Howard Johnson orange roof would make my mouth water for a mocha chocolate ice-cream cone. But my color palette has shifted. Possibly because my hair is no longer blond I don't look as good in orange now. Also, I tend to get circles under my eyes when I'm tired, and orange washes me out. I lived my orange period fully and am happy now to experience orange in touches. I have an orange tree in my office that gives me great joy; I have an orange lacquered pen Peter gave me that reminds me of cantaloupe. Some of my porcelain fruits are orange. I put oranges and lemons in a bowl and it is very satisfying. But now I prefer peach tones to pure orange when I buy clothes and when I decorate, because peach is softer.

YELLOW: A PRIMARY

The color of day, sun, light, and expansion, symbolizing air and earth, radiating warmth. Yellow is the most light-giving of all hues, symbolizing bright hope and expectancy, activity, energy, joy, and incentive. Yellow is youthful light and the color nearest white light. Yellow has the brightest chromatic intensity of the three primary colors (red, yellow, and blue) and symbolizes spiritual enlightenment. Christ ascended to heaven in a glory of yellow. Yellow is also honor, health, and well-being. It is the lightest bright color, suggesting cheerfulness and radiance. Yellow cars have fewer accidents because they are easy to spot. Like red, it is a stimulant and has an energizing effect, but is lighter and less dense; it is more suggestive than stimulating.

Yellow increases our metabolic rate, so we give off greater glandular secretions, providing us with energy and incentive. Yellow is sensuous and symbolically welcoming. Yellow is also the color of intellect, intuition, consciousness, and self-development. When someone is smart they are considered a "bright" wit.

What do you think of when you visualize yellow? I think of brilliance, radiance, and splendor, of spontaneous enjoyment. Yellow is fun, the happiest color—with the sunniest disposition. Sunshine, bananas, lemons, polished brass! Spring flowers—forsythia, primroses, crocus, daffodils, dandelions, and buttercups! Egg yolks, hollandaise sauce, butter!

Yellow is associated with sun, warmth, also the new and modern, the unformed future. The ancient Greeks bleached their hair yellow. In China during the Sung dynasty yellow was the imperial color, reserved only for the emperor. A recent test in the U.S. showed that young schoolchildren instinctively selected a yellow crayon to sketch a happy story and a brown crayon to sketch a sad one. All children paint a yellow sun.

My mentor, the interior designer Eleanor McMillen Brown, used to say, "Every room should have a touch of yellow." In 1928 she painted her drawing room walls a fresh shade of yellow with white pilasters and she hasn't changed the color once over the past sixty years. "When you get it right in the first place, why change it?" Think how ahead of her time she was to have picked such a clear, crisp yellow sixty years ago. Many people make the mistake of using a gold color when they paint their walls, which has the opposite effect of a light, fresh yellow. Yellow paint should have the inner glow of sunlight when used as a wall color, to suggest spaciousness, because it has the highest reflectivity of all colors, radiating outward to expand space. Four walls of a golden mustard color become heavy and dull. When black is added to yellow it turns a sickening greenish color and loses its brilliance.

On the other hand, vibrant polished gold sparkles with reflectivity and has vitality and inner light. Gold is the symbol of sophistication and the measure of earthly wealth. Gold is the symbol of the beyond, the kingdom of sun and light. Think of the pleasure we get from polished antique brass and from wearing antique gold jewelry.

Recently I chose for a couple's penthouse living room, dining room, and hall overlooking the terrace a Fuller O'Brien Fulcolor Free Spirit Yellow, the exact color of a pale daffodil. I wanted to paint the ceiling Faith Blue and the trim in a sparkling Swedish white enamel paint called Emalj. The wife loved the yellow color and her husband thought the sample too pale. We all met at the apartment and I had the painter open the can so the clients could see how the paint looked pure and wet—a delicious delicate yellow. I'd been in Connecticut working on a house that morning and my client had picked for me a host of daffodils from her cutting garden. I had brought one giant pale daffodil with me to the meeting in New York and I held it up to the painted wall sample. "Your walls will feel like this flower." My clients were persuaded, and the three painters began at once. The color is perfect. We found a green-and-yellow silk-and-linen French flowered rug and it goes beautifully with the pale yellow background of the flowered chintz we also selected.

Each time I walk into that apartment I immediately remember being six years old. We lived in a large eighteenth-century house on top of a hill on a dead-end road. Above our land was a huge field which was the highest point of land, and we could see Long Island Sound easily from this favorite play spot. In early spring something magical happened on this field—

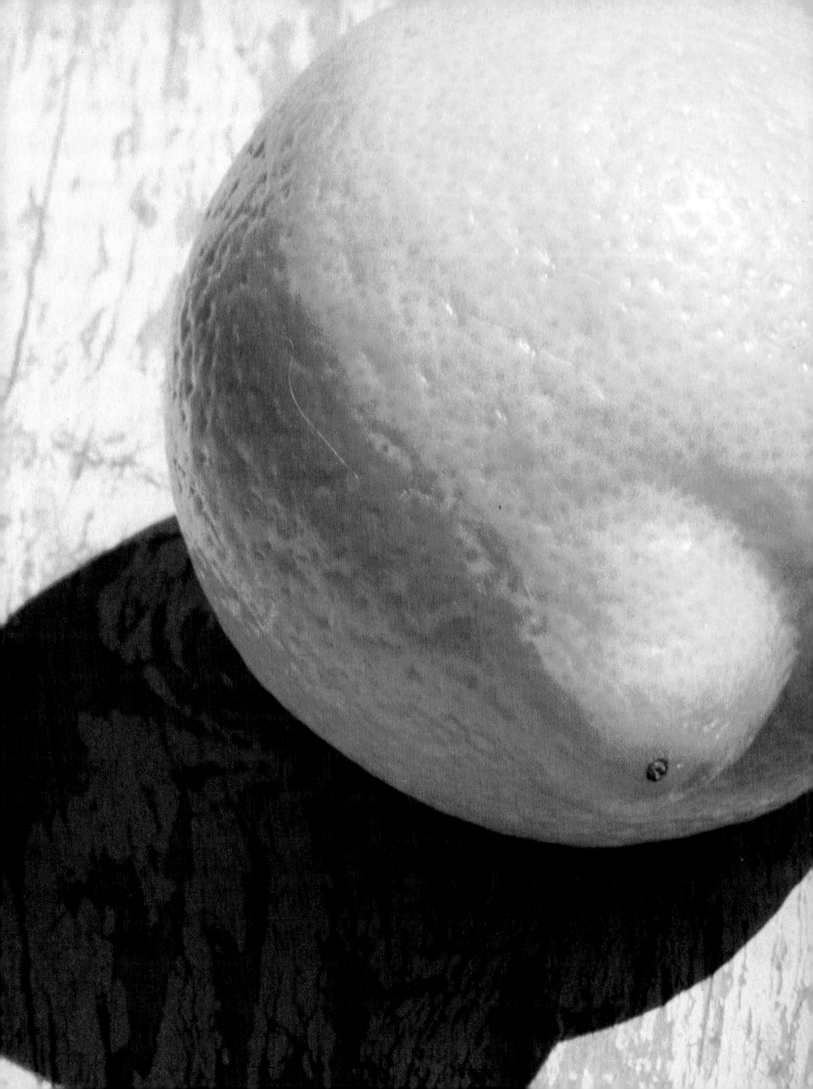

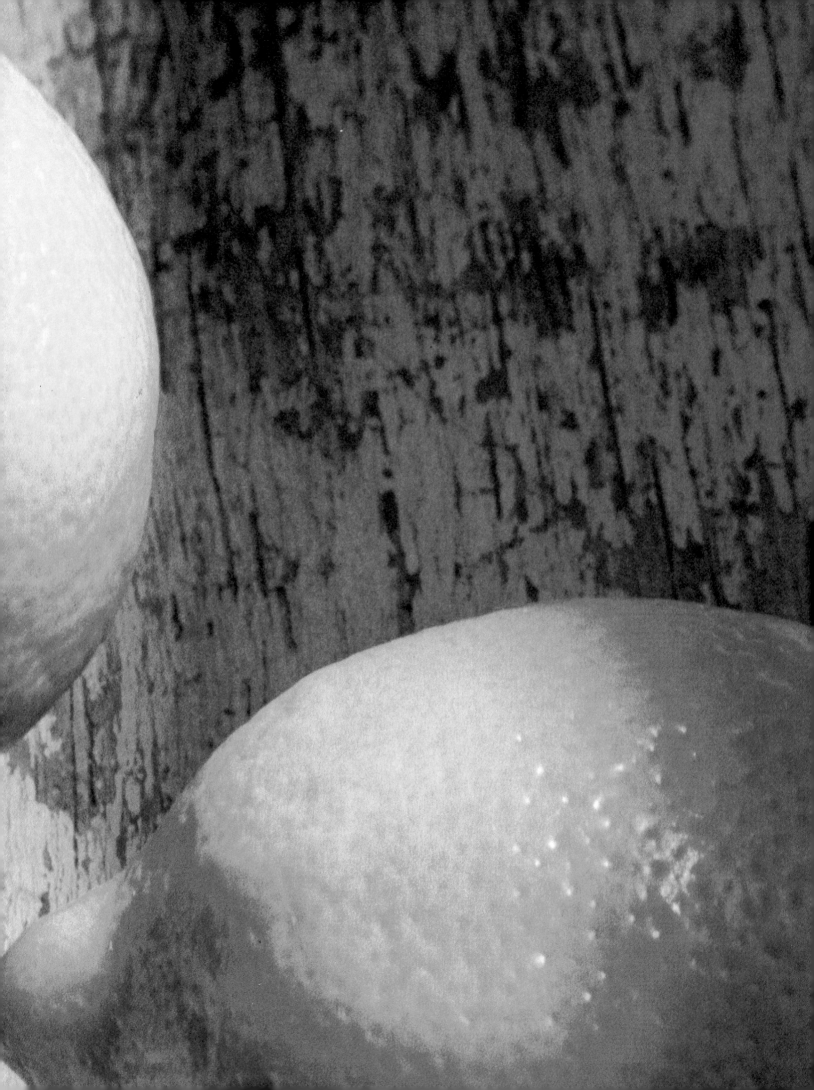

thousands upon thousands of yellow daffodils would blossom and the air smelled of spring.

No one ever came to this field except children, and unless you were right up there on the top of the field, you couldn't see the daffodils because they were camouflaged in tall grass. The sight was breathtaking. This penthouse apartment on Fifth Avenue with a garden terrace brings me back to the miracle of spring on that special hill in my childhood.

When Peter and I were married I moved into his Park Avenue apartment where he had lived for twenty years. The first thing we did was paint and decorate to make a new and very personal color statement. We had *no* view, and knowing that yellow is a cheerful color, and because of all my pleasant associations with yellow, I painted our living room walls yellow. They remained yellow, about the shade of Eleanor McMillen Brown's, until I left her firm and started out on my own. I'd seen the extraordinary wall painting workmanship the French are known for in Paris while I worked on an eighteenth-century house there, and when it was time to freshen up our paint I had the walls lacquered to bring in more light and changed the yellow wall color to a pale peony pink. The soft hue was created by putting a few tiny drops of red inside a gallon of Emalj white paint. What I didn't realize until after the fact was that the peony walls were a more gentle transition from indoors to the brick building across the way.

But I'll never outgrow my love of yellow, and all of our upholstered furniture is done in a cheerful yellow chintz. Van Gogh was obsessed with yellow. Yellow is radiantly cheerful when contrasted with dark tones. Our yellow chintz has rich dark greens. Do people get a yellow streak because they're afraid to use yellow?

GREEN: A SECONDARY

Green, a combination of blue and yellow, is the most popular of colors because it is the most restful to the eye, and is considered so basic it is a "psychological primary." Green is a symbol of the mysteries of life, of green pastures. I give it the same importance in decorating as the three pure primary colors, red, blue, and yellow. Green symbolizes sensation, balance, normality, water, and earth. Green is the color of Epiphany, the birth of a new year. It is a dominant nature color, representing fruitfulness, the vegetable kingdom, and the mysterious chlorophyll involved in photosynthesis. Robin Hood's cloak was green. Green is the color of young growing crops. Green expresses hope, tranquillity, contentment, knowledge, faith, and constancy. Until Elizabethan times the bridal gowns in England were green to express fertility and hope. It is cool, evoking tranquillity and peace. Green is astringent, luminous, and refreshing; clear water often has a green hue. Green is young leaves, grass, ferns, trees, moss, watercress, jade, malachite, and emeralds. Early glass contained iron, which gave it a green tint. Green is limes, peapods, spinach, parsley, asparagus, and artichokes. Mint. Green is Key lime pie, pistachio ice cream, lime crush, and menthol-fresh.

Green is new buds and nature in perfect harmony. Green was my maiden name and my mother used green ribbon in her typewriter. Green is also the color of healing and accord, because it gives a relaxing effect both physiologically and psychologically. People who like green are deep-

rooted and proud, socially well-adjusted, interested in self-preservation; they're civilized and conventional. Green means "Go."

In the eighteenth century in France the Sèvres factory created a distinctive green, *vert pomme* (apple green). In the nineteenth century Paris green, a poisonous emerald color made from copper acetoarsenite, killed people who spent time in rooms where the color was in the wallpaper. It later became an insecticide used on locust swarms.

Studies indicate that people who are in a predominantly green environment have fewer distractions and a better ability to concentrate. When I decided to paint my little white study a rich hunter green my decision was based on intuition—I had just decided I wanted this room to be dark green. What I now realize is that white expands the room and I wanted a cozy, comforting place to go, where I could shut the door and write undistracted. My small home office, on the other hand, the place where I pay bills and prepare office work, is painted red. Green suits one kind of work, red another. Hunter green is an excellent color for a library or a writer's hideaway. I use an abundance of green in decorating because it helps to harmonize and blend other colors—just the way it does in nature.

BLUE: A PRIMARY

The color blue is a universal favorite among adults. Egyptians were particularly fond of blue. How do you react to blue? Are you true-blue? Blue symbolizes air and water. Although never actually named in the Old Testament, blue represents the physical and spiritual life—your existence!— and loftiness and depth. Blue has symbolic associations with royalty. Blue blood means highborn. Blue reduces blood pressure and heartbeat and breathing slows down. Dark blue is calming and quiet, passive and tranquil, and is the color experts advise as the most suitable environment for peace, contentment, and meditation. Blue represents tranquillity, self-contentment, self-moderation, and sweetness. Blue symbolizes harmony, unity, and balance.

Do you think of sapphires and lapis lazuli? Or Texas bluebonnets, forget-me-nots, periwinkles, and bachelor buttons? Do you think of Little Boy Blue? Blue is considered to be peaceful and relaxing, a symbol of nightfall and rest. Quiescence. It is also associated with winning. Blue stands for the best—first prize is a blue ribbon. Blue-chip means high quality. The blue poker chip means high value.

Depending on where blue is used, its effect will be different. In a mental hospital, blue walls have a calming effect. When the same color was used in a café, however, a study showed that the employees complained of the cold! Blue gives the impression of orderliness, awareness, and sensitivity. Blue represents faith, trust, and integrity. Blue is the color of silence. The poet Johann Wolfgang von Goethe wrote in *On the Theory of Colors* that we like to look at blue, not because it presses on us, but because it pulls us after it.

There is a negative side to blue which means sadness and depression. These are extensions of positive traits. Cool becomes cold, solitude turns to isolation and contentment to inertia. Washington Irving, in 1807, used "blue" in a story as an expression of despondency, for the first time abbreviating the older term, "blue devils." Yet when we sing the blues it actually gives us relief and pleasure.

The negative side of blue is a natural sorrow. "I feel blue." Picasso's blue period (1901–4) pointed to life's inherent sadness. The expression "blue Monday" refers to the Monday before Lent, when there was an alcohol excess preceding Lenten austerity. "Blue" meant tipsy. The Puritanical "blue laws" governed the sale of spirits on Sundays in New England.

The expression "blue self" meant righting your character. Ultimately the color blue points to the transcendental and heaven. The Romans linked blue with black—the final surrender, or relinquishment. To the Chinese, blue symbolizes immortality.

But blue skies are a universal cure for the blues and blue is fundamentally a healthful color. In Persia, turquoise is the national color and the gemstones are called *piruseh*, which means joy. Blue represented Jupiter and Zeus.

Josiah Wedgwood performed thousands of recorded experiments with the color blue, made from the expensive mineral cobalt, which became known as Wedgwood blue and for over two hundred years this pale, tranquil, dignified color has been a bestseller.

Ultramarine was produced from lapis lazuli and was used for illustrating manuscripts which cost as much or more than gold. Indigo blue was the first color to be synthesized.

For me, blue has been an acquired taste. As a child growing up, there was never any trace of blue in our houses except for touches of a dense dark blue in some oriental rug runners in the hallways. My mother believed blue to be a depressant and she wanted the house to be warm and cheerful. I love the water and beaches, and sunny days always have blue skies. The painter Kandinsky wrote about blue as an "attractive void." I began feeling comfortable decorating with blue when I worked on a beautiful vacation house in Palm Beach and all the colors were shades of blue and blue-green. Even the mirror over the mantel in the living room was blue cut glass. Twenty-five years later I feel that blue is a real friend and I remember with fondness doing a huge house on an island off Connecticut in shades of the sky and water that brought in rosy pinks from the sunset as accents.

Our library in our New York apartment used to be a dense oriental red color inspired by a red lacquer picnic basket my mother had brought me from Japan. It was a good, rich color for a library. When our daughters became teenagers we needed a room where they could entertain friends, listen to music, and watch television. We transformed this room into a beach house atmosphere by painting the walls fresh white and the ceiling a soft sky blue, and by using a crisp blue-and-white chintz on the cushions of the natural wicker furniture and on balloon shades at the windows. The coffee table is lacquered an intense, rich evening-sky blue and the floors are bleached a sandy color rubbed with a little white paint which takes away the reddish cast. To add sunshine to this cool, refreshing hideaway, we painted the wall behind the bookcases daffodil yellow. The other tables and chairs and an antique English high piece are all faded antique pine. The use of blue in this room along with an informal mood gives one the impression of being on a terrace overlooking the beautiful waters of Bermuda. Several years ago I was in the David Findlay, Sr., art gallery looking at paintings with some Greek clients for their house in Patmos and my daughter

Alexandra stopped by. She spotted a Roger Mühl painting of sky, water, and a rooftop in the South of France. She fell in love with this painting and later Peter and our daughter Brooke joined us at the gallery. We all agreed—this predominantly blue painting hanging over the sofa in our blue-and-white library would give us the impression that we were in a beach house on the water.

Our kitchen walls were once white rough plaster with chocolate-brown cabinets reminding us of a French farmhouse kitchen in Provence. Now, our kitchen has white rough plaster walls with shiny Brittany-blue cabinets! After years of living with the brown, I felt it was too dark and dense for our family. We found a company in the Yellow Pages that custom-matches paint colors in a special spray for appliances. Our dark-brown stove, dishwasher, and refrigerator were transformed into a lovely soft Brittany blue. Imagine walking into your kitchen to make coffee and prepare breakfast and feeling as though you are on the rocky coast of Brittany! It is a breathtaking room both by day and by night. We have hung on the walls many small lithographs and paintings in shades of blue painted by Roger Mühl in Brittany.

Contemplating blue soothes us and has a pacifying effect on our central nervous systems. Blue calms space and atmosphere, so when you feel a need for nature, tranquillity, and peace, especially in an urban environment, blue can feel wonderfully peaceful and transcendent. Blue gives space a feeling of infinity.

I wear a lot of blue. One of my favorite dresses is bright blue with large white polka dots. Blue is flattering to nearly everyone. People who are overweight like dark blue because it is slimming. Years ago we could only find navy blue in shoes, belts, and accessories. Now, with the synthetic of the aniline dyes and coal-tar derivatives and metallic oxides, plus silk imported from China, we have a huge variety of intense clear colors to choose from. Blue is a favorite color for clothing for young people and young adults. Think of blue denim. Blue accepts dirt more gracefully than other colors. Blue is the color of working life—blue-collar workers. My favorite pen is an intense blue Waterman called "Le Lady," which I found in Paris several years ago.

Blue is still the most popular color for a bedroom because of its calming effect. I've discovered that some of my clients are collecting blue-and-white Chinese export porcelain. Many people are creating predominantly blue rooms. To keep the room from being monochromatic (one-colored), they choose yellow or rosy pink or blue-green accents to create a warmer, more interesting blue palette. Vasili Kandinsky, the abstract expressionist and color theorist, teaches us that blue has a tendency to get deeper. Blue is cool and tame, and refreshingly calm.

VIOLET: A SECONDARY

Spectral violet is the shortest wavelength, and violet light has the highest energy. Violet is a mixture of red and blue, which are opposites on the color wheel. Violet has some of the impulsiveness of red and the surrender of blue and symbolizes sensuality. Purple has a heavenly delicacy and richness. Mauve enjoyed a vogue in the mid-nineteenth century because it was taken up by the fashion-conscious French. Magenta, the reddish-blue color named after an Italian village, overtook mauve. But purple has had a checkered career. Some think purple can be orgiastic and ostentatious. Cheap. Vulgar. It is the color of power, and power corrupts. In ecclesiastical symbolism the purple robe is worn for sacred activities; it expresses the mystery of the Lord's passion and the power of the spirit. Identified with the Easter period, especially Ash Wednesday, purple was also the color of the robes worn by the Roman emperors—the "imperial purple." Why, after the nineteenth century, when few things were left in their original state, did purple develop such a bad reputation except among a chosen few? Was it a reaction to the fact that violet had been available only to priests and rulers?

In psychology a preference for purple indicates internalization and sublimation and suggests depth of feeling. Once you become captivated by Van Gogh's purple irises—an emotional burst of iris in a white pitcher, painted in 1890 in the last months of his life—you become lost in a garden of purple irises and may remember spending time appreciating your own purple irises as a child. Monet would invite friends to visit him when his irises were in full bloom at Giverny. What would we do without hyacinths, irises, violets, lilacs, and lavender? Violets were medicines in medieval times. The oils of violets are still used as perfumes. Violet is a medieval color term, and purple, an older term, got its name from the ancient Tyrian shellfish used to obtain dye centuries ago.

Purple may have its virtues, but they do not guarantee its continuing popularity. Less than twenty years ago the late Mrs. Brunschwig, of *Brunschwig & Fils*, the famous international fabric house which sells exclusively through designers, wouldn't have purple in any of the thousands of fabrics she sold in her line. A study showed that purple was the fourth favorite color of both men and women in 1941 and in 1969. But to her, purple was vulgar.

I was asked to design a table setting for Gorham Silver Company in the late sixties and I came up with the idea of weaving together colorful ribbons—in plaids, stripes, polka dots—to make a tablecloth. My inspiration came from pansies. I used a variety of different purples and strong yellow

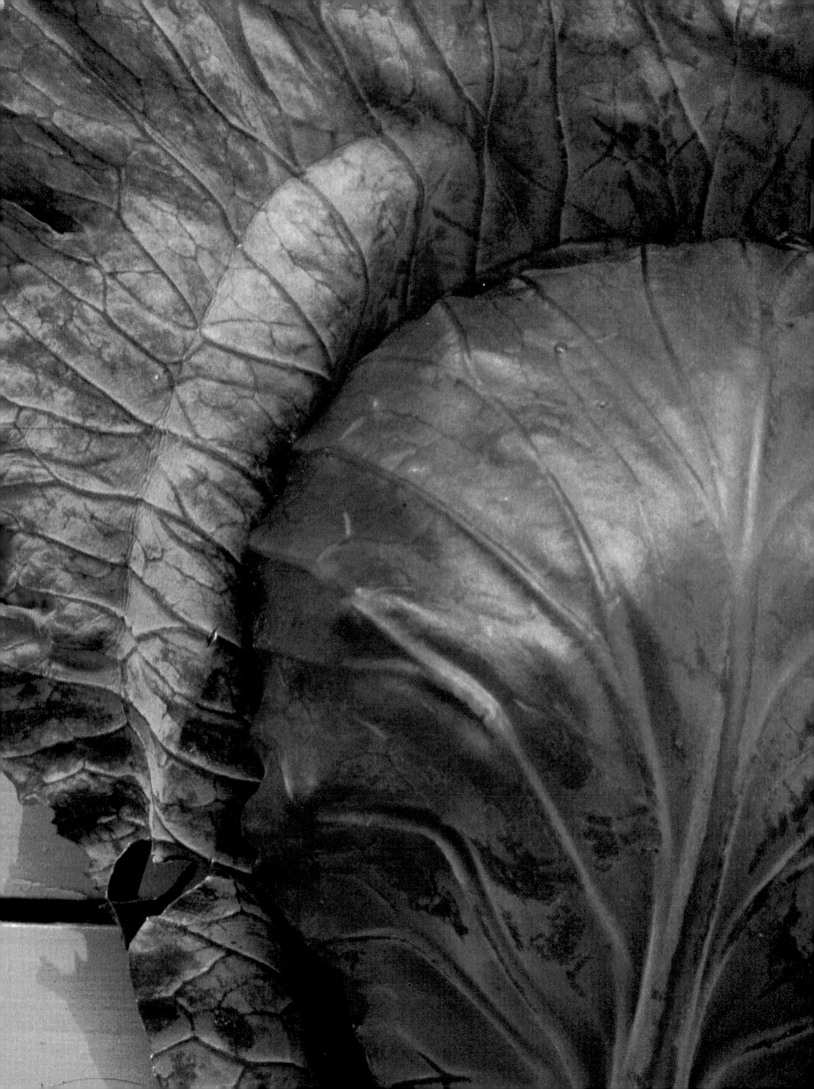

mixed in with greens. It couldn't have been prettier, and after the exhibition I took the design to Mrs. Brunschwig and asked her if she would be interested in printing the fabric and having it in their line. She took one look at the tablecloth and said, "We'll print the design, but you'll have to come up with some other color combinations. We can't have purple!"

For those of taste and style, purple was the color to laugh at. Friends would inquire, "What do you do when you take on a new client and they love purple? Do you tell them you can't work for them? Or do you tell them purple won't do?" As I write, I am using purple ink, have a brass watering can on my desk filled with lilacs, and holding my writing pad is a lilac clipboard, reminding me of June nights on our sleeping porch in Connecticut where lilac bushes hugged the screen porch. When I see violet I smell lilac blossoms. The scent of lavender reminds me of my grandmother. There are approximately 50,000 acres of lavender in France. Once you experience the violet light of the breathtakingly beautiful south rose window at Notre Dame, you are spiritually transformed. My book *The Postcard As Art* was printed in two colors, one being lilac. I have a lovely amethyst egg on my desk to pick up and stroke when I need soothing. Amethyst meant "not drunk" in ancient Greece and was a love charm that helped people to sleep. Shakespeare wrote of Cleopatra on her barge: "purple the sails, and so perfumed that the winds were love-sick."

III

YOUR PERSONAL COLOR

PALETTE

STEPS TOWARD FINDING YOUR PERSONAL COLOR PALETTE

*O*nce you take firm steps toward developing your own color palette, you won't be concerned with what colors are "in" and what colors are "out." When you establish strong memory associations with your happy colors and color combinations, be true to yourself. The colors you are attached to are necessary for your sense of wholeness, equilibrium, and happiness.

You and I must realize that other people's color sense and color palettes may have a negative influence on us. Our parents, our spouses, children, friends, our boss, fashion designers, interior designers, what's available in stores, what's displayed in advertisements have lured us to go along with current trends or to excavate colors from an earlier period in history that are not personally understandable or emotionally important to us. Paint companies hook up with historical landmarks to sell us paint for our homes that may be inappropriate and meaningless. In many cases the original vibrancy has been clouded over with dirt and age and we are sold tired copies of color associations. You and I have to discover our own color visions. And that requires becoming physically involved.

YOUR COLOR BOX

The first step toward discovering your own color palette is to select a pretty colorful box. It can be a large hatbox or a clothes box—the color and shape are up to you, but it should be roughly 10 × 14 × 4 inches or bigger. This will be your color palette box. What color do you want for your box? Did you select a solid color or a pattern? A friend of mine picked a Florentine marbleized box in pink, yellow, blue, and green. Another used a glossy green box from a department store. Find a ribbon that coordinates with your box for an added touch of color. My box is covered in a blue marbleized paper with a blue ribbon. Put colors that delight you in this color palette box. Toss in the lining of an envelope a friend sent you. Throw in a delicious melon-colored Jordan almond if this luscious color makes you happy. Add a piece of patterned wrapping paper or a snip of yarn, a swatch of fabric or a button. Or the shell of a robin's egg. Don't be concerned with how these bits and pieces of color will come together. You can always combine color and circumstance later.

The point now is to play with color and understand that the color puzzle is a lifelong process and passion, not something to solve and forget about. For instance, one friend asked for a snippet of carpet from a château she stayed in in the South of France. She was certain this was the color blue she wanted for her own bedroom when she redecorated. When the time came, however, this wasn't the blue she selected from her color box. She'd found another, clearer blue in the interim and that was the blue she used.

These color fragments should fill you with nostalgia and private delight. Toss in a candy, a leaf, a dried flower, a marble egg, or a ribbon. Go to a paint or art supply store and select color chips that appeal to you—don't worry now if the yellow you select will be your living-room walls or a bunch of daffodils in a clear glass pitcher. The appropriateness of circumstance will guide you when the time comes to make a color decision. If you worry about suitability now, you will never fully develop your passion! Fall in love with what colors you see and capture them for your color box.

Most of us have no *true* color memory. Unless we have samples to match up and compare, we can't make an accurate color judgment. Interior designers and architects always bring their samples with them in order to examine them in daylight and compare. Never be casual about any color. Be exact. "A little off" is an unnecessary compromise and will be disappointing. Be strict and put only your most treasured colors and hues in your color box. If you find a scrap of patterned fabric that you like and it has twelve different colors, if there is one color you don't like in the design, cut out the good part and *throw away the unwanted color*. Never compromise.

ALEXANDRA STODDARD'S

Put in a few favorite-colored pencils and crayons, a few postcards by artists you admire where all the colors speak personally to you. Rip out colors from magazine ads and pictures. Artists and designers get their inspiration this way. Your *own* color palette will be original because of the way you combine and harmonize your favorite colors.

This very personal color box will intensify and electrify your understanding that you now have the power and ability to color your life immediately and beautifully! Through intuitively selecting colors that you know are emotionally uplifting to you, you will create a world of happy colors that become you and represent you.

Get in the habit of making every color a personal choice for your color box. Let no one else judge or guide you. Never ask a friend or helper what they think of a color you like. It's self-defeating and not relevant. First you want to learn to choose colors straight from your heart. If you like to paint, make some color samples from your favorite pure tubes of paint. Mix in white and create a variety of intensities. Once you begin this personal creative process, you will discover you are expressing strong feelings in these choices and you open yourself up to see everything around you in a new light. Look around you now. Are there any possibilities to add to your color box? Children tend to gather their favorite things instinctively. We don't want to get bogged down wondering where to put things we love to touch and see. Through the use of your private color palette box, you will

freely be back in touch with the freshness and wonder of your happy childhood memories. Add things to your color box that will trigger your memory—Necco Wafers, gumdrops, a tiny candy conversation heart. A matchbox from a restaurant, a seashell, a pebble, a scrap of fabric, felt, a piece of mica, wood, metal, a feather. A photograph.

How long will it take you to fill your color box? With luck, a lifetime. You'll find that you're more on the lookout to make new discoveries because you have a specific place to save these revealing clues. And over time, you'll find yourself weeding some colors out. What you once thought was a wonderful pink will be superseded by a new find.

You will see that so many of the colors you adore are not pure primary colors, or even secondary colors, but combinations of the three primary colors of red, yellow, and blue.

While we think of colors of the spectrum as bands of color as seen in a rainbow, color experts have created color circles. The most basic one has twelve colors.

These twelve colors, made by combining the primaries and secondaries in specific proportions, constitute the basic "color harmony wheel." You can buy a color wheel color key made by M. Grumbacher, Inc. (estimated price, $4.00) in most art supply stores. This is a handy tool for checking which hues work together. It shows you the colors you can create by adding

           ALEXANDRA STODDARD'S

other colors plus analogous harmonies and complementary harmonies. Feel free to break rules and always trust your judgment. I adore violet and yellow, but when these two pigments are mixed together they produce an ugly green-brown color. Yet if you put violet and yellow irises together in a vase it is beautiful. Having a guide helps you to see your color development. I suggest you pick up a color wheel and put it in your color box. Delacroix, the nineteenth-century artist who was actively concerned with color problems all his life, kept a color wheel on the wall of his studio. All colors can go with their neighboring color; all shades from the same family—whether greens, reds, or yellows—can be used together. Match up your favorite colors from your color box with the color wheel and you can see your own color palette emerging. You might discover that you enjoy complementary colors in some circumstances, and it is interesting to chart your own color evolutions. Hold each color up against clear white. Some of my friends line their color boxes with white tissue paper so they always have white as a background for their colors. I keep a pad of pristine white paper in my color box so I can easily test my colors. Study each color for clarity, luminosity, and life. Because white is light and energy, you will want the colors you select to be refreshing so they will give you a vital lift.

YOUR OWN BOOK OF COLOR

Next, make your own book of color. Look around in your bookcase or in a bookstore until you find a large picture book that seems the ideal size and shape for your personal color book. I recommend a book about 10 × 12 inches. At an art supply store buy large sheets of thick white glossy paper and have them cut to size. For example, shiny oak tag comes in 28 × 22-inch sheets. Begin by buying a dozen sheets which can be cut to make forty-eight book-sized sheets. Select paper in your favorite colors from a color matching system. Pantone is an excellent color system with a collection of 747 colors called Pantone Color Specifier—The Pantone Library of Color. In New York City, the art supply store Sam Flax carries the full Pantone line. Pantone sells a less expensive swatch guide that can be an invaluable aid to identifying basic colors you like. Each Pantone color has matte or glossy paper to match. Pantone indicates formulas to teach you how to mix these basic colors to create your ideal tints, shades, and hues.

Buy some Pantone sheets—they come 20 × 24 inches—in your favorite colors and cut them to the size of your color book. If your color book is 10 × 12 inches you will have four pages to every sheet; if you by a dozen Pantone sheets you'll have forty-eight colored pages. Combining these with your white papers, you will have a gorgeous color book of ninety-six pages. Keep your book sheets loose so you can add to them and take away at whim. Your color book then becomes a portfolio. It is fun to spread out all your sheets as you work on your color book. Cut two thick sheets of cardboard, one for the top of your book and one for the bottom. Then decorate the front cover and endpaper with a favorite marbleized or patterned paper. Tie the length and the width of the book with a $1\frac{1}{2}$-inch colorful cloth ribbon as if it were a present. To keep your color book clean and safe, store it in a beautiful box. Keep your three color boxes together as your personal color library. This will inspire you to add to them on your continuing color journey. Eventually, you'll discover pairs for all the beautiful pictures you've collected.

Next, clip out of magazines and catalogues everything colorful that is visually appealing to you. Edit what you don't like—crop pictures and photographs to suit you. Be irreverent. This will be your private one-of-a-kind color book. (This is the precise method I used to prepare my own book of color.) Store all the materials for your own color book in a sturdy, colorful box, making sure that it is several inches larger than your book size. The box that holds the supplies for your color book should be approximately 4 inches high. Just as it is valuable to keep all your color samples in your color box, you need a safe place to put all your color book materials. You may decide that these two color storage boxes can be the same size.

Here's how I created my own color book. After gathering thousands of colorful images of gardens, beaches, living rooms, bedrooms, bathrooms, and terraces from seed catalogues, food ads, art and auction catalogues, and fashion and shelter magazines, I then began to separate them into color schemes. I took off my glasses to allow the colors to merge, creating the effect of an Impressionist painting, and I separated the color images into logical color categories. What I discovered was that all my favorite pictures of man-made things have a parallel in nature. My theory that nature can be our color teacher held up beautifully.

I put four general categories together—The Garden, The Seascape, A Walk in the Woods, and The Colors of Food—then paired up these images until I found relationships that were startling. For example: a blue-and-white tiled bathroom with lots of mirrors can be juxtaposed with a shed with a blue door all covered with snow. Or, with sparkling-clear blue water and sky at a beach. Place side by side the visual images drawn from nature that relate in color and spirit to your interim room scenes. The colors we are innately drawn to are colors we loved earlier in our lives—some of us

first understood blue at the beach or under the rich blue sky of the plains, and our love of flowers aroused our love of clear, delicately fresh colors. Or, because we may have crunched through snow in red boots as a child, we understand the joy of snow and are not afraid of pure white. We have seen the reflections of snowflakes and color tinting the snow and we know the same magic can happen in our own home. If we use mirrors architecturally to add light, they will create reflections in much the same way we may have experienced the reflections of color on a frozen pond where we once ice-skated or on the surface of the water as it laps the shore.

We learn about our own colors by paying attention to how we react to the colors we experience around us. Take these images and inspirations from nature and pictures of man-made settings and put the associations together into the categories of your choice. Create pleasing layouts showing nature as the inspiration behind decoration and design. Show a waterfall with cascading fresh water tumbling down rocks surrounded by moss and wildflowers. Then pair it up with a bathroom that has green glazed tiles surrounding the tub. Show a beach with sky, sand, and water, and juxtapose it against the interior equivalent—a peaceful living room in shades of blues, blue-greens, and white, with sandy bleached floors. Have a picture of a farmer's market and then show a buffet where the corn, tomatoes, peas, and peaches are presented for a family meal.

EVALUATING THE COLORS THAT SURROUND YOU

Now that we have begun to collect for our color boxes and have spent time with our color books, let's step inside the rooms where we live and take a look at the colors we see. Be as objective as possible. Go from room to room with a pad of paper, a pen, and your color box and stop to analyze what each room's color message is.

First look at the overall color statement of a room. Is the room light in feeling or is it dark and heavy? Does it cheer you up or make you sad? We will change the colors of our surroundings throughout our lives and when we do, we should use color to nourish our spirit. For instance, our brown kitchen was heavy and dark and dragged us down even though it was charming. So we changed the color. When I go into my green study I want to concentrate and tune out the rest of the world. Because that is the purpose of the room—the dark green pleases me and the rich color is appropriate. Just looking at our living room puts a smile on my face. If you

ALEXANDRA STODDARD'S

have a baby, go into the nursery and experience the atmosphere. I've discovered that I've never outgrown the gentle, fresh colors of my childhood and I seek them because of their power to delight my spirit. In other words, the colors of a nursery, if they personally please you, don't have to be limited to that one room.

Continue your tour through your home, noting your reactions on your pad. Note what pleases you as well as what you'd like to change.

When you open up to your honest reactions to what you see and feel, this is the first giant step toward making where you live express your own color palette. When we dig inside ourselves for the truth, we're not hurting anyone's feelings and, so far, it isn't costing us any money. How do you react to the color of the dining room table? Is it heavy and dark or is it elegant? Let your eye absorb the whole and also analyze each detail room by room. Study the color of a chair, a footstool, a plant container. How is the lighting? Are the colors harmonious? Is the feeling restful? Welcoming? How do they work as a whole?

Think of each room as a painting. The colors you use for each room

should be thought through carefully so your favorite colors are successful when put together. One red flower vase could be a high note to a room. Interior designers use color as a tool to transform a room into a feeling, much the same way an artist applies color to his canvas. We begin by deciding on a color scheme the way an artist sets up his palette. How do you want a room to feel? If you say, "Light, expansive, and sunny," you begin with the thought that the colors will be on the bright, vivid side of the spectrum. Envision a garden and think of trellises, grass, sunshine, and flowers: green, yellow, and pink.

See where you have remained true to your color palette and where you got lost. My French country kitchen had been selected by *House Beautiful* as the kitchen of the month when it was brown, and it was admired by everyone who came into our apartment. Yet it wasn't my color palette and therefore it didn't give me as much pleasure as it now does with Brittany-blue-painted cabinets.

Rooms that work have a color scheme. Choose two or three colors you want to mix together. Be strict about not adding too many colors at first. Sue loves blues and rosy pinks. Nancy likes fresh pale pink against dark hunter green. Kathy enjoys peach, cream, and soft greens. The reason each color scheme is successful is because of its simplicity. A room that has a specific color message is refreshing and also restful. Edit your colors so that you have no more than three per room. For example, yellow, pink, and green; or lilac, green, and pink; or blue and yellow. Rooms that are washed with white woodwork and trim give your color scheme space to breathe. Most rooms have wood floors and furniture, so once you choose your ideal color scheme, determine what wood tones will complement it best. If you want everything to be light and fluffy, choose to bleach the wood floor and have some of your furniture painted or pickled with a light strain so it isn't too heavy in feeling.

What I learned from having brown kitchen cabinets was that everything in the kitchen was brown or tones of copper brown except the white stucco walls. The baskets, copper pots and pans, maplewood countertops, cork floor, antique farm table, and rush-seat chairs were all brown! Even my wooden spoon collection blended in with the rest of the kitchen. Although I had a bowl of apples, oranges, lemons, and limes on a table and colorful chairs and napkins, the room lacked color and life. The only time it came alive was when I'd put on a vivid floral apron and start slicing tomatoes and shucking peas out of pods, steaming spinach, or cooking shrimp in the wok. But a room should also be colorful in repose.

Be daring with the few colors you select for your color scheme. When you add wood furniture, books, paintings, and other objects, your pure colors will be toned down and become background. Mahogany, for example, sings next to pale yellow and pale green. Colors are never seen in isolation; they are part of a complex whole.

The biggest color mistake is to select muddy, musty, dusty colors. It is one thing to go to a museum restoration in Deerfield, Massachusetts, or Williamsburg, Virginia, and see the rooms painted in colors that are from two hundred years ago. The rugged life of the American frontier—with the mud and the soot from the candles and the constant smoke from open hearths—has little relationship to the way we live today. In many cases, even with limited pigments available there were originally vivid colors that have grayed down and faded with age and heavy wear and tear. The gilding in Versailles, for example, was brilliant when it was first applied; so when it is restored, the curator makes it gleam.

Live in your own color time. Technology gives us many impersonal advances, but when it comes to color, today you can have any color you can imagine. Let clear, luminous colors age naturally with time. Begin fresh. If you don't want strong colors, select pale clear colors tinted with white.

Another common color mistake is to throw too many patterns together.

My mentor, Mrs. Brown, taught us to repeat shapes and colors to gain harmony. Her living room walls are yellow with white pilasters and trim, and her upholstered furniture is yellow damask with touches of white. Antique chairs are accented in apricot cut velvet, and as the crescendo focal

ALEXANDRA STODDARD'S

point she has a Venetian red lacquer high secretary. The yellow walls, yellow curtains, and repeated yellow upholstery color give her room air and space so the eye doesn't have too much to take in all at once. You can use several different subtle patterns, but each one should add harmony to the composition.

When choosing patterns, have one scale predominate. If you use chintz, for example, the other colorful patterns should be minor notes on the keyboard so they don't compete with the rhythm of the chintz. Remember that a room has architecture, scale, form, and dozens of different proportions, shapes, and details. Use color to harmonize all these different elements. If you have a chair that is a bit awkward in scale and shape, you can make it blend into the room gracefully by putting the same fabric on the chair as you use on your sofa and other upholstered chairs. On the other hand, if you have a sweet Victorian tufted slipper chair and you want it to become more prominent, cover it in an accent color picked out from the chintz and repeat the same fabric on several seat pads.

Think of each of the rooms where you live as a type of music. Your living room might be classical and your kitchen jazzy. Each room can sing a different tune as long as you join them together with white painted woodwork. White painted moldings, doors, and baseboards allow rooms to open up generously, one to another, connecting the different personalities of each room into a unified, organized whole. With the exception of a wood-paneled library and possibly a dark red or green room whose walls and woodwork are the same color, paint all the architectural trim white. Only the flat wall surface receives color. Ideally, you will have one white you use throughout your house. If, for example, you decide to use a red and off-white toile fabric in your study and you paint the walls the same background color as the background of the fabric, have that be an exception. All the rest of the house should have a purer white trim like the Swedish enamel called Emalj.

Let each room sing a specific subtle color song. Use strong accent colors in small doses. If you have a yellow chintz that has eighteen different colors in it and one is red, when you isolate that red and put solid red pillows on the chintz sofa the red could shout at you. Study the chintz. The red is used in touches. Never force a color. Rather than having aggressive red pillows, try red tulips in a clear crystal vase. The red contrasting against the green leaves will be strong enough and infinitely more subtle. Or, perhaps you have a small Chinese red lacquer picnic basket or a red painted tray you can place on a table. A charming room smiles at you, but never screams.

Color depends solely on light. Have light-catching objects. Polish the brass banding around your wooden bucket. Polish the brass hardware on your table. A crystal obelisk displays the spectrum of colors when a beam of sunlight passes through it. A crystal ball lets colors reflect back at you.

A shiny surface reflects all available light and brightens a room. Mirrors bring light and double the colors reflected in them. One bouquet of daffodils becomes a "host" when placed in front of a mirror. Use mirrors architecturally to bring in more light and view.

Color is your tool to transform the limits of space in bad weather and darkness and assure you a cheerful place to go that refreshes you. The colors should have an inner glow, so that when you are not in your best mood or the weather is dreary, you can turn on the lights and feel cozy in your rooms. Feed your color sense when you feel wonderful so it is there to surprise you when you're having an off moment. Color each room to fulfill personal needs. If you live in a city and miss having a garden, turn your rooms into interior landscapes in full bloom. Have green plants and trees and some flowering plants and cut flowers. Remember that through color you can always keep your rooms alive and vital.

By changing a painting or rug you can give a room a different character. Be attentive to the seasons so your rooms change as you do. When you feel your house looks dark and gloomy in the winter solstice, put a bright,

ALEXANDRA STODDARD'S

colorful quilt on the hall table or hang one on the wall of the stair landing. In the spring when the weather brightens, put a huge vase of quince blossoms or forsythia on the bare wood of the hall table.

Color is alive and ever-changing. You see and appreciate colors best when you change them around so your eye is caught by surprise. Have reversible pillows so you can change the mood of your living room by turning them.

Consider having a summer scheme. Pick up all your rugs. Slipcover your upholstered furniture with inexpensive sailcloth or mattress ticking. Move your paintings around so you have an opportunity to appreciate each one in a place of honor—say, over the mantel or the hall table.

Seasonally strip each room of small objects and put them in one place as inventory. With a fresh eye, put things back room by room in a new way. You will discover that so many of your possessions have a similar color message. By moving small objects around it is possible you will appreciate them more. Blue predominates in our library, kitchen, and bedroom. By moving colorful favorite treasures around, I am refreshed in my sensitivity and color awareness.

Next, open up your closets and study the clothes you wear. How do specific colors make you feel? Study the different tones you wear in different seasons. Look at your silk scarfs (or neckties), your shirts and bathing suits. Examine your hair ribbons, aprons, linen napkins, dish towels, and pot holders. All these little things are additional clues. Open up your linen closet and examine what color palette you see. Are there towels, sheets, and blankets you don't enjoy because of the colors? Evaluate what colors you adore and what colors you would like to weed out. Next, open up your refrigerator. Is there anything inside your refrigerator that is a color you particularly like? Oranges, apples, lemons, limes, raspberries, or cherries? In my book *Living a Beautiful Life* I suggested creating an attractive still life inside your refrigerator by using see-through storage containers. Another idea is to store cut flowers inside the refrigerator and bring them out when you're home and can enjoy them. In this way, when you open your refrigerator the garden colors you adore will be the first thing you see.

COLOR MAGIC

Whether you make color changes immediately (by changing the napkins you use or by painting a wall), or make notes about things you want to do to improve the colors around you, you are on your own color palette path. Pull out every drawer. Look in every cupboard. Be on a personal color hunt. I have a friend who believes each of us has our own special color.

Hers is a soft pink. I have several favorites—pink, yellow, lilac, robin's-egg blue, peach, cool pale blue, white, soft green, like the leaf buds of early spring. See if you can find your color(s) in the most humble, hidden places. Note whenever you find a color that offends you. I find I can't have a rag

in my rag drawer in my laundry room if I don't like the color. I've discovered that a dreary rag becomes something I avoid touching. A worn-out pastel towel, cut up, can be a rag I enjoy using to dust or polish. The same goes for garbage bags. White with a yellow cinch cord is refreshing. Examine your ironing-board cover, your clipboard, your mailing envelopes, list pads, your marking pen, storage boxes, and scissors. Every object that surrounds you and makes up your world can enliven you with *color*.

EDITING COLOR

All of us have too much haphazard and random color in our lives. Some came as gifts, others are phases we went through that no longer apply. It is not appropriate to add more colors to what we already have. First we have to eliminate all the *negative* colors in our immediate surroundings before adding fresh, clear, positive colors. Once we do this we can build on the ones we've grown to like. . . . Take a new look at your napkin and dish-towel collection. Examine your pottery and china. Study everything from pots and pans to hats, shoes, wrapping paper, and the color ink you use. *Everything tangible around you is a color* that has an atmosphere for *you* alone. All these things are clues and they are the everyday ordinary things that make up our daily lives. If you are willing to *reject* some colors and combinations you currently aren't enjoying, you will be providing space for what you truly relate to as your own life-enhancing color palette—a color wheel you can live by.

Resist using a paper clip if you don't like the color. If you buy a package of mixed-colored paper clips, separate the colors you like from those you don't like. Do this while making some necessary phone calls and you'll be amazed how much more patient you'll be when you are put on hold. Immediately something rather ordinary can become a powerful color statement because it has your color point of view. Eliminate, say, orange, black, and brown from red, blue, yellow, and green and both batches become punchier. Combine red and blue and yellow and green. A rainbow of random colors is not just meaningless, it can be vulgar. I edit colored pencils, tissue paper, M&M's and just about everything where I have a color choice. Have you ever counted the different colors of jelly beans? There are forty different colors and flavors, and I separate them into several (what I think are) attractive combinations! The ones that don't harmonize with my schemes are edited out. Knowing their names is fun, too. Some of my favorite colors and flavors are cotton candy, Island punch, Mai Tai, ice-blue mint, pink grapefruit, cream soda, and lemon-lime. What do I do with my rejects? I find someone who has a different color palette and give them a tiny gift!

It's fun to personalize colors down to the lining of a kitchen drawer, to the color of your exercise mat and leotard, to a ponytail tie. Elastic bands come in geranium red, lemon yellow, and azure blue. Erasers come in cheerful colors, too. One color touch that frustrates me is decorated paper towels and tissues. Why ruin pure white? I select postage stamps that have attractive colors. If I buy a sheet of mixed stamps and some are prettier than others, I use the best-looking stamps when I write to my friends and use the others to pay bills. I read that Perry Ellis did the same thing—there was a series of stamps several years ago featuring lilies and he selected a specific one for some invitations he sent out and the others were used "back office."

MATURITY

As you search for the colors you respond to positively and edit out the colors you realize you no longer appreciate, don't be embarrassed if a color your really don't like is one you've lived with for twenty years. Be determined to express your individuality and originality through your passion for particular colors and combinations. What you envision now as your color palette is what matters. You know that the right colors will enhance the quality of your life. I have gone through the most amazing color phases and I know that we all do. So unburden yourself and let go of colors that no longer please you. Start weeding out a room at a time or try the most inexpensive things first—for instance, bathroom towels and the pads you use.

A study suggests that the favorite color of 75 percent of preadolescent schoolchildren is violet. And yet few adults put violet at the top of their lists. The point is that you will go through many color chapters in your life. Live each one with flair and imagination. Experiment and edit. If we don't admit to our changed reaction to color we will never fully mature and develop to our full potential. The fun is to use color intimately and immediately to express ourselves as we evolve and grow, so our personal colors bring us more and more pleasure each day. If you look at the lining of your sewing basket and it looks sad, you can instantly transform it into a lovely color simply by tacking in a cotton napkin you like in shades of pink and lilac, or a scrap of lime-green material left over from your bedroom curtains. Sort through your button collection and your thread collection. Why live with colors you loathe?

AVAILABILITY

Today, everything you could ever want can be found in the colors of your choice. Manufacturers offer over 12,000 hues (not including black and white) for wall paint, rugs, fabrics, place mats, tablecloths, towels, sheets, stationery, and clothing. Never before has there been such a variety of good color combinations and availability. For color dazzle, look at the large silk scarfs sold at Gucci and Hermès. I believe we are becoming more aware than ever before of the importance color plays on our mood, attitude, and spirit. We have a wealth of colors to choose from. So go to it, always keeping in mind that we want to select our own colors and integrate them into a palette that satisfies our souls.

Once we create our own color palette box and our own book of color, color becomes more alive, an extension of our essence. It is no longer mysterious and elusive, but a real part of us. Colors have a heartbeat and they breathe. Colors change with the flick of light, and with the interaction of other colors. When we get our own color palette right, we often experience a physical reaction in our solar plexus that involves our whole being and satisfies our physiological needs. Color perception is a function of the brain and when you get the colors right—to the eye of the beholder—you will feel great delight. This is a sensuous, emotional moment—highly charged, fleeting and beautiful. Once you discover firsthand that every color you experience has the power to dramatically alter the way you feel and can

open up your imagination, then you'll understand why your own personal color choices are paramount. The color refills in your Filofax, for instance, make a difference. That may sound silly, but think about it. If pink gives you a lift, why not turn to pink a couple of times a day rather than to white. Likewise, use color to code your different projects. In this way your file folders, your pen, your pencils, your sheets and towels, your bathing suit, hat, socks, sweaters, earrings, coat, your dinner plates, blankets, quilts, bedspread, your bathroom wall color, tiles, the grouting of your tiles, your hand soap—these physical things become instruments to carry out your color message; they become tangible symbols for you of a very meaningful expression. According to Dr. Max Lüscher, the color theorist and creator of the Color Test that reveals personality through color, colors are the mother tongue of the unconscious.

Think what your life would be like if you didn't pay attention to color, if you didn't have the opportunity to experience the joy of color in food, in the landscape, in decoration, in clothes—think how flat and dull life would be. By comprehending color through the rewards of experimentation, the results can be spectacular and we will be doing justice to our individuality. Focus on the beauty of color that is available to you each day so you won't be missing one of life's greatest gifts. We are living in an age of color and we should continuously work to raise our color consciousness. Color is freely given us to as a tool to shape a richer, more beautiful life.

SENSITIVITY

Color appreciation takes time to acquire, like art or music appreciation. But unlike art or music, color can be studied wherever you are, whatever you're doing, because everything in nature and everything made by man has a color. We are surrounded by color. The most modest, routine daily rituals can be color lessons. After a rainstorm, when the sun comes out, go outside and look for a rainbow. Have you ever seen a double rainbow? The next time you take a bubble bath, ponder the magic of the color spectrum reflecting on each bubble. The next time you go to a farmer's market, concentrate on the joy these colors bring you as you select eggplant, apples, pears, pumpkins. Buying and preparing food—eating a meal—can teach us about color. Looking out a window at the view, sitting inside by a fire, going to a movie, shopping for household supplies and clothes, walking in the woods or down the street—things we do each day can teach us more about color. Stay alert to what color is saying to you. We have to listen and embrace our affirmative reactions. Look for light refracted through a crystal object, a diamond or a chandelier. Notice how one color plays against another to influence it and alter the way you see. The pure white cornice molding in our living room looks like pale sea-foam green, for example, because it is reflected against lots of mirrors, the peony walls, and the yellow chintz. I'll never forget taking a shower in the tropics once in a "garden shower" where the sunlight made the cascading water a rainbow of color. I enjoyed the warmth, the sun, the water, and the dazzling spectrum of color.

EXPERIMENTING WITH COLOR

Go back to a favorite garden and examine the colors. The next time you're arranging flowers, experiment with some of your favorite colors from your color box and use flowers to represent your colors. Begin to collect small colorful objects for your home. In time you will discover that many of your objects can go from room to room and be compatible and harmonious. When you buy new towels don't buy all one color—select three happy colors from your color box and use them together. Try raspberry, lime, and yellow—or pink, grass green, and lilac—or yellow, peach, and apple green. Some weeks use only two of the three colors. One week use all raspberry or all green. Mix things up so you are awake to the *different surprise effects of the colors that are affecting you emotionally*. If you enjoy patterned sheets, change patterns every other week so you have a color change. I am an avid quilt collector because of the extraordinary color magic of the patterns and I use different quilts on our bed each week to add color dazzle.

Don't always try to balance your colors evenly in a room. One color should make your color statement and the rest should be there as support. One of the prettiest rooms I've ever been in is a library in Old Westbury, Long Island, painted a penetrating dark blue with a blue-and-white toile cotton print at the windows and slipcovered on the furniture. One bowl of tulips—yellow, white, orange, and plum were the color accents. Fabric designs should have an even flow of color. The Italian fashion designer Emilio Pucci used shocking, thrilling, raw pigment, but notice that he has the brightest color in the smallest amount, and that it is evenly distributed throughout his design. When I created my pansy-inspired ribbon design and translated it into a tablecloth, I used the same ribbons vertically and horizontally to give harmony and balance.

You are in complete charge of coloring your own life. If you get your color palette right, you can have a happier, healthier, more emotionally

balanced and satisfying life. By never taking color for granted, you will live in beauty.

Always carry good-sized samples of your fabrics when shopping. All professional designers do. If necessary, it is better to buy a yard of fabric and live with it in daylight and at night that buy a bolt and be disappointed. Artificial light can change coloring completely. Look at your coordinated samples together in daylight and ponder their associations. Experimenting with color samples costs little. The magic of color is that we can change it if we don't like it.

Sleep on colors you are envisioning. Mull them over. Let them grow on you naturally. Leave color and come back to it and then decide. Let color get inside you.

SPONTANEITY

Color is the cheapest and easiest form of change. You can control the colors you experience to a larger degree than many people realize. Never live with a color you don't like. If you outgrow your love of your hall wall color, you can spontaneously eliminate it and replace it with a luscious color you adore. I always ask for white or light pastel-colored hotel rooms when I travel, and I have extra lights installed in the room before I arrive. I've stopped going to certain restaurants because I don't like the colors they

use. I'm particularly disturbed when I'm in the tropics and the restaurant chooses orange tablecloths combined with lots of dark wood, which unfortunately reminds me of Halloween. Years ago I bought some wild sheets on sale—lilac, black, green, and white—and I couldn't wait to go home to make my bed up in my new sheets. At first it was exciting, but after reading in bed for a while I turned out the lights and couldn't sleep all night! The sheets were so aggressively colored and patterned, I had bad dreams. That was a real lesson to me. I should have started out small—bought a pillowcase and tested it. When selecting color, take time to consider personal subtleties of shade, hue, and value. Buy a pint of paint and make a generous sample before you paint an entire room. Study the color in daylight and at night, on sunny and dark days. We should experiment until we find an ideal balance—not too strong a hue, not too weak and light, but just the right color saturation and balance so combinations of favorite colors enliven us and warm our hearts.

Each day, look at color with fresh eyes. Be appreciative of the delicate miracle of color vision. Think of the Impressionists and how much fun they had mixing colors and experimenting. They spent days studying colors from nature. We know they painted over some of their canvases, and some they destroyed. I am reminded of a Metropolitan Museum mother-child art class I took with my daughter Alexandra when she was two. Mothers sat at grown-up tables with a two-inch brush and the three primary colors plus white. Our two-year-old children sat in front of us on little chairs at low tables with the same ingredients. The two-year-olds were at one with the colors and they splashed them on their white paper with a combination of happy exuberance and riveting concentration. These children experienced joy while they played with the magical colors. The mothers hesitated and waited before even dipping the brush in the delicious pure paint. They looked at each other in embarrassment, hesitant, halting, not willing to take a chance, to commit. We should all try to regain a childlike wonder so we can continue to experiment with colors all our lives. If you feel inhibited, buy some fingerpaint and have some fun sitting on the kitchen floor enjoying the wonder of color.

When my daughter Alexandra discovered at age two how to make purple by adding blue to red and mixing white, it was a revelation to her. And when she found out how to make pink by adding red to white, she announced, "I want these colors in my room." Alexandra has lived her twenty-one years in pinks and purples. Looking at pictures of her in her purple, pink and white bedroom when she was three and four reminds me that we create our own world once we discover color as our magic tool. Because we in her family know how much she loves purple and pink, we are all on the lookout for sheets, quilts, posters, and fresh flowers that nurture her passion for her color palette. Pink roses are her favorite flower,

so she does have these associations from nature, and has rose-scented potpourri and a pink Rigaud candle that smells like a profusion of pink roses on a hot July afternoon. Stepping into her bedroom is like having tea in a gazebo surround by a pink rose garden.

COLOR YOUR LIFE
WITH BEAUTY

Color instructs us to open our eyes and hearts to a wider vision. When we put colors together and create our own color palette that lifts us spiritually, we are a part of creation. Think of your color palette as an ever-widening harmonious circle, always expanding to include the subtleties and mysteries of colors you like. There will be many beautiful colors in your life and the more beautiful they are, the more glorious your happiness will be. Beautiful colors are the language of a radiant life.

IV

A COLOR

JOURNEY

THE GARDEN

As an interior designer I have realized that all of the pleasure and beauty we have experienced in nature can be transported inside. Nature can truly be our teacher. I invite you to take a color journey with me now, first into the garden.

We can bring a garden-soaked color palette into the homes where we really spend most of our lives.

ALEXANDRA STODDARD'S BOOK OF COLOR

ALEXANDRA STODDARD'S

ALEXANDRA STODDARD'S

THE SEASCAPE

*The colors we are innately drawn to are colors
we loved earlier in our lives — some of us first understood blue at the beach.*

ALEXANDRA STODDARD'S

ALEXANDRA STODDARD'S BOOK OF COLOR

ALEXANDRA STODDARD'S

ALEXANDRA STODDARD'S

A WALK
IN THE WOODS

A walk in the woods can awaken us to the warm
beauty of the pine, oak, maple, or fruitwoods we live with every day.

ALEXANDRA STODDARD'S

ALEXANDRA STODDARD'S

ALEXANDRA STODDARD'S

ALEXANDRA STODDARD'S

ALEXANDRA STODDARD'S

ALEXANDRA STODDARD'S

COLORS FRESH
ENOUGH TO EAT

Certain foods are richly colored — strawberries, spinach, corn, canteloupe, asparagus, tomatoes, carrots, watermelon, eggplant, oranges, blueberries. This intense color association — along with the wonderful tastes and textures — doubles the pleasures of eating.

ALEXANDRA STODDARD'S

ALEXANDRA STODDARD'S

ALEXANDRA STODDARD'S

ALEXANDRA STODDARD'S

PUTTING YOUR COLORS
TO USE

"To paint is to bring color to its maximum intensity so that it becomes vibration and light."

—ROGER MÜHL

TIPS ON COLOR

- The freshest, purest, cleanest white paint is a Swedish enamel called Emalj. The purer your white, the more beautiful the colors near it will tint it.

- Place colors in order of sequence. White, gray, and black are harmonious. If, however, you put white between black and gray, your eye jumps and the combination becomes irregular.

- Stick to simple hues—red, orange, yellow, green, blue, and violet, which go well together, and tint them with white.

- Stretch your color palette to avoid neutral tones. The opposite of pure color is gray. Do as the Impressionists did and use pure colors tinted with white.

- Beautiful colors are not out there: they are inside our brains, in our minds, experienced in our hearts, and seen through our eyes.

- When combining colors, hues that make the best tints are normally light in value when pure. Add white to any light color on the spectrum— yellow, yellow-orange, orange, green, yellow-green—and it will be pure and clear.

- Take any hue that is normally dark in tone—red, red-violet, violet, blue-violet, blue—and add black. You will create a pleasant, rich color—an excellent choice for a library, study, or powder room.

- Pale yellow, peach, crimson red, and deep violet look good together because you tinted the light colors (yellow and orange) and shaded the dark colors.

- In decorating, try to have all your paint colors pure and tint them with white when you desire pale hues. Try to avoid adding white *and* black, which tones down the freshness of the color.

- My favorite color harmonies are always pure saturated color, tint and white. These are flower colors from nature.

- If you want to separate two colors so they won't fuse together, use pure white or black. For instance, if you have pale pink walls and an Atmosphere blue ceiling, paint the cornice molding white.

- Yellow never changes hue when lightened with a pure white. When black is added to yellow, it turns an ugly green tone and is depressing. Always keep yellow fresh and pure. Add white only.

- Any hue in a certain color scale will harmonize. Add white in equal proportion to any hue and the colors will be pleasing together.

- The greatest color contrast possible is achieved by using the complementary or opposite color. Complementary colors make the strongest, most vivid color statement. Green, the complement of red, is dramatic when placed next to red. Think of red Christmas balls hanging on the branches of an evergreen tree or of Van Gogh's intense pictures using these complements.

- When any two colors are side by side, because of an optical illusion they appear to change hue; this effect, first discovered by Leonardo da Vinci, is known as simultaneous contrast.

- When you see green in a grid outlined by gray (gray is darkened white, which reflects the whole spectrum), the gray appears to be purple, the complementary color of green. This effect is called the after-image phenomenon.

- Whenever you place gray next to a hue, the gray will appear to be tinted by the complementary of whatever color you use. Gray next to blue appears to look brown because the complementary of blue is yellow.

- When you want a pale tint, always add the colors to white. The smallest amount of pigment can alter the hue of a color. It takes a large amount of white to lighten a color. For black to become pale gray, for example, it takes 99 parts white to 1 part black. Study the Pantone color chart and you will see some colors are *50 parts white to 1 part color hue*.

- Taste is a matter of personal preference. Blue and green used together have been given a bad reputation, yet look at water, a green lawn, and the blue sky. Do as the Japanese have done for centuries: use the color combinations in nature for your designs and schemes.

- Each light wave is a different hue. The human eye sees between 180 and 200 colors in the spectrum. Each hue emerges with a distinct personality. However, it is human to seek simplicity in the complexity of the world of color. Test yourself: how many different colors can you visualize?

- Each color varies according to its degree of saturation and its ratio of lightness to darkness.

- Give more importance to warm colors than to cool ones. They are more dramatic and lively because the eye sees more warm colors than cool ones.

- Color is our tool to express our self-image.

- The clothes we wear are seen more by others than by us. The colors we decorate with are seen most of the time by ourselves.

- Each of our senses responds to a particular form of physical energy. The stimulus for vision—seeing—is light. Light is electromagnetic energy. Color results from light waves.

- The rainbow (the spectrum of colors seen by the eye and experienced in the mind because of light) is a symbol of peace.

Colors for Rooms

- Blue recedes and is an excellent choice for a bedroom, where you want to feel calm and peaceful.

- Because many of us occupy smaller spaces, the best advice is to keep most of your wall colors light.

- Each room in your house or apartment can be a different color and still harmonize if they are separated by white woodwork. For instance, a living room can be lime green, a dining room pale raspberry, and a library a dark winter green.

- Yellow is an excellent color for halls where there isn't much daylight. This is a good color for a front hall because it's a fresh color to come home to.

- Pale Atmosphere Blue is a great color for ceilings because it expands the space to give the impression of infinity. This is especially nice in a bedroom so you can lie in bed and gaze up as though at a pretty sky.

- Rooms that face north tend to look and feel cold because they never get direct sunlight. Light, pale tints are best for these rooms. Recommended colors are yellow, peach, and pink.

- Primary colors stimulate and enliven the mind. They look best in sunny, south-facing rooms, tempered with splashes of pure white trim. Recommended colors are red, yellow, blue and greens.

- White is by far the bestselling paint color. Light bounces off white surfaces. Shiny white surfaces create airy feelings and open up space. Sparkling white reaches out and overflows boundaries.

- Yellow needs strong light to look bright. and if there is no light (as in hallways), use a pure yellow because the walls and floor will shade the color. For example, Fuller O'Brien Fulcolor paint color Perfect Yellow is ideal. This color can be lightened by adding white.

- Remember that the color you select for walls will be seen in shadow, and the rug color and surrounding upholstery fabrics will affect the wall color. Keep your wall color a pure tint. Use a pure color plus white. Color automatically tones down when applied to a vertical surface because it appears in shadow, and the floor, ceiling, and adjacent walls reflect color and tone on each wall surface.

- Black reads as a heavy, containing solid color. Use it in touches—for a lacquer screen or a coffee table.

- Cool wall colors will slow down circulation, so you actually feel colder in a cool-colored room.

- White paint with a few drops of red creates a pale pink color for walls. It's stimulating and gives a lovely, healthy glow to face tones. In a living room, where we spend time in conversation with friends, this is a good color. If you live in the country the pink will look attractive contrasted with green grass and trees. In the bleak of winter it will feel warm and glowing. In the city, pale pink walls look good when the view overlooks other buildings—limestone or brick. The transition between indoors and out is gentle.

- If you see a blue-green carpet you like in a room in a French château, get samples that are a close match and try them out in your house or apartment. The light will be different, but artificial lighting can adjust the difference. Always look at colors in their exact location and study them under both natural and artificial light.

- Color is light. If you have a room that doesn't have a lot of light, don't use too dark or strong a color on the walls; and find ways to have lots of white. Install a chair rail and paint it white. Add ceiling molding and paint it white. Hang a wallpaper that has white stripes and a color so that 50 percent of the walls are white, which is light.

- A room that is used mostly at night—say, a dining room—should be light and cheerful when seen during the day or it will appear depressing. If, however, you have a dining room that is isolated from the rest of the house and it is used for candlelit dinner parties, a rich, saturated dark color can enhance the mood of elegance and romance.

- Always use warm incandescent light that closely resembles daylight. Experiment with pink- and yellow-toned light bulbs. You need light to see color and feel its energy.

- Gather all your favorite colors. Decide which color you want to use to unify your rooms. Maybe you will use a green-and-white rug in the living room, hall, and dining room because you want a clean sweep. If the living room walls are, say, a wide spring-green and white stripe, your rugs will join the living room with the dining room though the two rooms have different-colored walls. Green is a good rug color because it looks pretty on brown wood floors, is practical, and brings in the feeling of nature and a garden.

- When pigments are mixed it subdues the power of the color. Select pure hues that have only white added to them.

- I prefer chintz patterns to solid colors on our upholstered furniture because they break up the form and soften the lines. Solids seem bigger.

- I like walls to be painted or to have a simple wall covering. Wall coverings with complex patterns are too busy to hang art on, and they become contrived and static in time. Art looks fine on stripes and small pastel geometrics.

- Floors in your rooms make up 35 percent of the visual effect. If you don't want to cover your floor with a rug, you can bleach it, stencil flowers and ferns, or stain it green or blue. You can spatter your floor or marbleize it, or bleach and stain the floorboards for drama.

Twenty-four
Color Exercises

EXERCISE 1: PLAY WITH COLORED PAPER

Buy twelve sheets of colored Pantone paper, two from each color in the spectrum. One sheet should represent a pure spectrum color, and for each color select your favorite hue and value of that color. For instance, red and magenta, orange and peach, yellow and pale lemon, green and chartreuse, blue and turquoise, violet and lilac. Play with these colors. Move the paper around. Study the relationships. This is a very contemplative exercise. Create harmony and discord by your placement of colors.

EXERCISE 2: DUPLICATE A FAVORITE PAINTING

Select a favorite painting and examine its colors. Then rip pieces of paper in these colors from magazines and make a collage that represents the spirit of the original work of art. You might select a Manet or a Monet or a favorite Matisse. You will quickly discover the subtleties of color and will train your eye to see in greater detail.

EXERCISE 3: RATE YOUR COLOR TASTE

Color is intimate; it affects us, like the air we breathe, immediately. It affects our emotions. Train your eye and mind to study colors and be sure you are consciously aware of your reaction. Never disregard contradictory subjective responses to color. Based on your instincts, not on what you know or don't know about color, rate colors. You might like a particular shade of apple green but are repelled by it when it is inappropriately selected for the color of a car. Express your color taste. When you experience something you really love, register this consciously—from one to ten, give it a ten. So much of life has a price tag attached, but this is not true with color. You are able to select colors you adore, rejecting those you don't like, and this process costs you nothing extra. Look around and see how the colors pass your color-rating examination. When your colors are ten, your mood will reflect a similar rating.

EXERCISE 4: READ COLOR THEORY BOOKS

There are many useful books that discuss the effects of color on our emotional state, and even our sense of self. But I don't believe in relying only on objective color studies, because they are highly technical and may play tricks. A particular shade of bright pink can calm a violent person in prison. The same shade of pink could make a healthy person neurotic. You have to internalize all the colors you are exposed to and analyze your own emotional response. Use these studies to enhance your love of color, to help you use color to produce aesthetic pleasures so that you will understand more about yourself and others. But never be intimidated by scientific theories. Voltaire thought Newton to be the greatest man that ever lived. Goethe thought Newton's color theories were "an old nest of rats and owls." Da Vinci experienced colors as representative of the elements: yellow—earth; green—water; blue—air; red—fire. Aristotle thought in terms of light and dark. Jung and Freud had their own color theories. Whether color appeals or depresses depends on your individual personality. When you work on your color palette you are simultaneously discovering secret clues to your essence. We are ultimately in charge of the colors we select. While every specific color has an objective, universal quality of stimulus, how you like the color, how much you desire a color, is individual.

Some of my favorite books on color and color theory are:

- *Interaction of Color*, by Josef Albers (Yale University Press). An artist's poetic explanation of color.

- *The 4-Color Person*, by Dr. Max Lüscher (Pocket Books). A book about self-realization through color.

- *On the Theory of Color*, by Johann Wolfgang von Goethe (M.I.T. Press). A philosophical, scholarly guide to the study of color.

- *Designer's Guide to Color* (three volumes) (Chronicle Books). Practical exploration of color through pattern.

- *The Lüscher Color Test*, by Dr. Max Lüscher (Random House). A delightful book that comes with eight color cards and reveals your personality through color.

- *Colorgenius,* by Steven John Culbert (Dell). Tells what your favorite colors say about you.

- *Color Me Beautiful,* by Carole Jackson (Ballantine Books). Describes your color season and helps you learn what colors flatter you.

- *The Art of Color*, by Johannes Itten (Reinhold Publishing Corporation). A serious study of color from an artist's point of view.

- *Principles of Color*, by Faber Birren (Van Nostrand Reinhold). Tells you all you'll ever have to know about color.

- *The Language of Color*, by Dorothee L. Mells (Warner Books). Reveals how the energies of color can enrich all the parts of your life.

- *Color & Human Response*, by Faber Birren (Van Nostrand Reinhold). Shows how light and color affect your well-being.

- *Theory and Use of Color*, by Luigina De Grandis (Abrams). An excellent visual guide to color.

- *The Artists' Handbook*, by Ray Smith (Knopf). A simple aid to the use of color for artists and designers.

EXERCISE 5: TAKE THE LÜSCHER COLOR TEST

This remarkable psychological test by Dr. Max Lüscher reveals your personality through color. Buy his useful book *The Lüscher Color Test* (Random House). You will find eight color samples that you simply arrange according to your positive response until each color is placed in descending order from your favorite to the colors you least enjoy. Then read his account of what your true personality is and why these colors represent you.

EXERCISE 6: ORIGAMI AS ART

These brilliant-colored papers come in squares of three sizes. Buy a package with the intention of creating your own Josef Albers color interactions, not to turn these squares into menageries of birds or flowers as the instructions suggest. A package has fifty-five sheets in three square sizes—8 inches, $5\frac{7}{8}$ inches, and $4\frac{1}{2}$ inches, in a wonderful range of colors: pale blue, intense blue, hot pink, pink, red, orange, black, brown, yellow, silver, green, melon, and gold.

Now play with these squares. Put a $4\frac{1}{2}$-inch yellow square on top of an 8-inch red square and stare at it. Place a green $5\frac{7}{8}$-inch sheet between the red and yellow. Make another of blue and red. Do the colors appear to look purple?

Buy some patterned origami paper and play with patterns and solids. Mix patterns together.

EXERCISE 7: MAKE COLORFUL CUTOUTS

Using a sharp pair of scissors, cut out colored paper in forms Matisse-style. I call this carving in pure color. Begin by pairing together complementary colors: red–green; red–orange with blue–green; yellow–violet with yellow–green; red–violet with orange–blue; yellow–orange with blue–violet.

Use your color wheel to help you select the exact complements of each colored paper. There is a lively optical effect in opposites where each heightens the intensity of the other.

Paste some of your forms together. Now you understand the pleasure Matisse had playing with cutouts.

EXERCISE 8: COLLECT ART POSTCARDS

My appreciation for color is always enhanced when I look at artists' color expressions—Matisse, Boudin, Monet, Manet, Cézanne, Caillebotte, Cassatt, Vuillard, Van Gogh, Morisot. We all have our favorites we turn to for inspiration. Think of yours. I find it refreshing to look at pictures of artists' work—at museums, in our apartment, at friends' houses, and in art books. Each time I focus on art and examine the colors I become freshly inspired.

Collect art postcards so you can study the color relationships at home after a museum trip. Carry them around in your pocket or purse so you can study the colors while waiting in line at the bank or at the post office.

Because the Impressionists were inspired by nature and changing light, I refresh my color delight daily by looking at nature through their artistic eyes. My book *The Postcard As Art* has thirty-eight original postcards from museums all over the world tipped into the book. What I didn't realize at the time I created my postcard book was that I was defining and honing my color palette.

EXERCISE 9: MAKE COLOR SHAPES

1) Draw a square and color it red.
   Draw a triangle and color it yellow.
   Draw a circle and color it blue.
2) Choose which shape you are most drawn to or
   which one you feel represents you.
3) Red represents passion.
   Yellow represents intellect.
   Blue represents spirituality.
4) Here you combine color and shape. Think of
   the color and shape that best fit you.

This exercise helps you to understand yourself better and helps you visualize form and color in combination. It will help you make easier decisions when selecting colorful forms for your home.

EXERCISE 10: PLAY WITH COLORED PENCILS

Buy loose colored pencils in all the colors you are drawn to and put them in a see-through glass. Keep this rainbow of colors on your desk. Play with the pencils—doodle, draw, make notes. Experiment. Get in the habit of using color, not a lead pencil, when you make notations. The glossy pencils will speak to you and you will be adding pleasure as you plow through paperwork.

EXERCISE 11: MAKE YOUR OWN COLOR CHIPS

With the leftover scraps of colored paper used for your color book, cut little $1 \times 1\frac{1}{2}$-inch pieces and put them in a see-through dish on your desk. Calm your nerves while on the telephone. Play with these colors. Arrange them and make designs.

EXERCISE 12: DISCOVERING OPPOSITES IN NATURE

Think of the color combinations in nature where opposites occur. Violet flowers often have yellow centers, and an orange sunset contrasts against a blue sky. Bring your color wheel with you as you go on a color hunt. Bay grape leaves are green and their veins are red.

EXERCISE 13: DISCOVERING THE ORIGINS OF COLOR NAMES

There were only six color terms to early man—red, yellow, green, blue, white and black. All other color names come from flowers, insects, animals, fish, birds, food, minerals, stones, and places. Make a list of these, leaving space to fill in color names borrowed from each category. Flowers = violet, lilac, orchid, magnolia, daffodil, peony. Food = peach, apricot, lemon, pineapple, lime, orange, chocolate, cantaloupe, cherry, olive. Places = Delft, Holland; Nile, Egypt; Tahiti; Chantilly, France; Siena, Italy; Magenta, Italy. Make your own lists.

EXERCISE 14: KEEP A COLOR DIARY

In a small notebook or pad, keep a daily log of the colors you've seen that have delighted your spirit. Each day describe some colors and combinations you saw. Do not put an actual color in your book—use words to paint the shade and special meaning of this color to you. This exercise is a helpful discipline so that you are always expressing your happy color affections. By describing a beautiful color you have seen, you actually double your pleasure. Try to match the color(s) you saw with your Pantone color swatch book and write the number(s) down. As you read over your notes, try to visualize the color(s) in your mind.

EXERCISE 15: SIMULTANEOUS CONTRAST

Place in a row five strips of a color, beginning with very pale on the left and graduating to the most intense on the right. Note the fluting effect where the tones touch each other. The chevron wood floors in my living room are two-toned and appear to have a third dimension where the colors touch.

EXERCISE 16: AFTERIMAGE

Make a five-sided black star and place a white dot in the center. Next to the black star place a black dot on white paper. Stare at the center of the black star for sixty seconds and then look steadily at the small black dot. You will see the opposite star.

The afterimage of red is blue-green, of yellow, violet. Stare at a sheet of yellow paper for sixty seconds and then at a sheet of pure white paper. You will see a pure, brilliant violet.

EXERCISE 17: COLOR ASSOCIATION GAME

On a clean pad of white paper list the following colors, leaving lots of space around each one: red, orange, yellow, green, blue, violet, brown, black, white. Think of free word associations and images that go with each color (you'll be drawing from the right side of your brain).

Some possibilities:

Red = Red Smith, hot, Boston Red Sox, scarlet geraniums, anger, ketchup, blood, Red Cross, stop, fire engines, flags, an early emperor's vermilion ink, danger, red wine.

Orange = fire, sunset, Orange, New Jersey; Orange, France; oranges, warning.

Yellow = sun, butter, daffodils, forsythia, lemons, the Yellow Pages, chicken, egg yolks, coward, the Yellow River in China.

Green = my maiden name, go, honeydew melon, springtime, a walk in the woods, pistachio ice cream, limes, grass, limeade, celadon, lettuce, mint, zucchini, a pond.

Blue = "something old, something new, something borrowed, something blue," water, sky, sapphires, blue ink, feeling blue, winner, baby boy, blue laws, lapis lazuli.

Violet = violets, lilac, lavender, grapes, hyacinths, pansies, amethyst.

Brown = my husband Peter Megargee Brown, Brownies, chocolate, coffee, patina of wood, mud.

Black = Mr. and Mrs. William G. Black III, lacquer, black eye, black ink, soot, blackboard.

White = lights sparkle, snow, waves, sheets, wedding dress, gloves, bleach, handkerchief, paper, canvas, stationery, vanilla, mashed potatoes, light bulb, nightgown, lily of the valley.

EXERCISE 18: ANALYZING IMPRESSIONIST ART

Go to a museum that has a large collection of Impressionist paintings. Study how this group of artists glorified the phenomenon of light by dabbing pure pigments on the canvas so that our eye would blend them to make an impression. Often whole paintings were completed at one sitting. The sketch and the completed picture were one. Go up close to the canvas and study the technique and then stand twenty feet away and enjoy the effects. Through the use of color alone, these artists represented the appearance of things under different kinds of light. Most Impressionists used pure color, tint, and white. Claude Monet is my favorite Impressionist because his colors are so fresh, clear, and natural. When he painted a shadow (which is the absence of light), the shadow complemented the colors of light. For example, the complementary of yellow sunlight is purple, so the absence of sunlight makes purple shadows. Monet was preoccupied with atmospheric effects brought by light at different times of day.

The Impressionists were intuitive about color, not at all scientific. Monet had a "horror of theories." Study Renoir's light dappling through trees on the skin of his models, and Seurat's optical mixing where two colors fuse into a third hue.

Study the enchantment of the cool, transparent blue skies and the warm tones of sunlight. Make some notes in your notebook or in a pad so you can use some of these magical color contrasts in your home.

EXERCISE 19: COLOR MIXING

Buy tubes of acrylic paint of each pure spectrum hue, some 1-inch brushes, a pad of heavy paper, and a large tube of white. This is a good basis for experimenting with color mixing and matching. Think of some favorite color images and experiment until you discover how to get that color by mixing paint. When tinting color with white, the color (say, red) might turn bluish, so add a touch of yellow when you add white. Create a lovely sky blue, lilac, spring grass, daffodil, peach, and baby pink. Have fun. After you've mixed these gentle colors, make a quick picture of a garden or a vase of flowers. It will be so fresh and pretty. You will discover that you will mix approximately 15 parts white to 1 part hue.

EXERCISE 20: USING FOUR COLORS, CREATE HUNDREDS OF COMBINATIONS

Select any four colors you like, such as yellow, green, blue, and red, and make a geometric design out of paper in which you use each of these colors. Select a zigzag or a series of triangles or squares within squares. Place the colors next to each other and then proceed to deliberately place them differently. The optical effects are amazing and the possibility of variety is endless.

EXERCISE 21: CREATING YOUR OWN COLOR DESIGNS WITH MARKING PENS

Buy ten to twelve chubby marking pens in your favorite colors and buy a pad of heavy white paper. Begin by making a pattern of stripes in orange and yellow. Then add accent thinner stripes in surprising colors. Small amounts of strongly contrasting colors will add punch to the colors. The smallest color change can make a big difference in the appearance. Notice how certain colors come forward and others recede. Place bands of green next to orange and the green will appear yellowish. Place a band of green next to purple and the green will appear bluer. This is the result of optical mixing.

EXERCISE 22: COLOR CODING

Color-code all your different projects. Use lilac file folders for one and yellow for another. Just as you avoid neutrals in your decorating, avoid them at your desk. Use colored mailing envelopes. Each day of the week send out a different color. Have your Filofax or data book color-coded so you have the pleasure of a rainbow of colors; each one will make you better organized. Have a different folder cover for each working day of the week— red for Monday, yellow for Tuesday, green for Wednesday, blue for Thursday, and lilac for Friday. Put airline tickets in your lilac Friday folder because you'll need them for the weekend. In your green Wednesday folder put the instructions for attending a meeting.

EXERCISE 23: GIVE PERSONAL NAMES TO ALL COLORS

Make up your own names for your favorite colors. Some people walk into my kitchen and think "baby" blue. I call it "Brittany" blue because I have happy memory associations. Baby blue means nothing to me.

Here are some of the color names I like. These are from the paint manufacturer Fuller O'Brien:

Angel Green	Blithe Spirit
Faith Blue	Far Away
Fragile	Free Spirit Yellow
Glo Blue	Kumquat Orange
Lime Twist	Magic Rainbow
Memoir	Memories
Alice Blue	Blue Radiance
Nantucket	Peaceful Valley
Twinkle Blue	Whimsical
Lemon Swizzle	Hope
Honeycomb	Mango Orange
Beauty	Laceflower
Plateau	Blue Island
Angel Wing	Blossom Pink
Apricot Nectar	Breeze Blue
Bleu Celeste	California Poppy
Celestial Blue	Clear Sky
Cool Breeze	Cornflower Blue
Southwind	Surf
Apple Blossom	Blue Surf
Wind Chimes	Water Mist
Secret	April Sky
Aqua Frost	Breakwater
Sea Foam	Ambition
Liberty Blue	Egyptian Green

You can make up names based on treasured memory associations—

Mykonos Blue

Cotton Candy Pink

Baby Spring Grass

EXERCISE 24: RAISING YOUR COLOR CONSCIOUSNESS IN A GARDEN

Go to a beautiful garden with a friend and take with you the Pantone color swatch guide plus your small notebook and a pen. Match up the colors you see in nature to your color guide swatches. See how many different colors you can identify on one flower. When you do this with a friend you will amaze yourselves with how many gradations of shade, tint, and tone you will be able to see. Give all the hues colorful names. Have fun!